Undistorted

God=Truth=Love

Copyright © 2022 by Kevin and Melissa Sheehan
Cover and interior design by Fritznel Elveus (www.elveus.com)

ISBN: 978-1-7350066-6-6

All rights reserved. No part of this publication may be reproduced, stored in a retrieval system, or transmitted in any form or by any means-electronic, mechanical, digital, photocopy, recording, or any other-except for brief quotations in printed reviews, without the prior permission of the publisher.

About the Author

Kevin Sheehan has a passion for pursuing spiritual truths. His desire is to share what he has learned about spiritual truths with others. That is the impetus for this book. Kevin has been blessed with seven children, the youngest three live at home with Kevin and his wife Melissa in Versailles, Kentucky. Raising children has been a tremendous blessing and source of joy for both Kevin and Melissa.

Contents

Introduction

Chapter 1   What Affects Our Belief/Unbelief in God?

Chapter 2   Spiritual Forces

Chapter 3   The Winning Power - God's Love

Chapter 4   God-Centered vs. Self-Centered

Chapter 5   Self-Control and Self-Discipline

Chapter 6   Healthy Life Habits

Chapter 7   Secular Thought vs. Spiritual Thought

Chapter 8   God's Will

Chapter 9   Heavenly Blessings vs. Earthly Blessings

Chapter 10   Reconciliation with God

Chapter 11   Life After Physical Death Occurs

Chapter 12   Spending Time with God and Miracles

Introduction

The reason this book has been written is largely because my wife, Melissa, and I are intensely motivated to bring clarity to the misperceptions that exist among humanity regarding who God is, who we are in relation to Him, what He expects from us, and how our obedience to Him affects our lives on earth and, ultimately, our life after we take our last breath. Melissa and I collaborated in thought regarding much of the content in this book, while I wrote the words. The concepts of truth contained in this book will reflect understanding, refined through study, of the source of truth, the Word of God.

Knowing truth and living truth are two different things. For example, let's say an astronaut described to you what it felt like to be in space, in zero gravity. Based upon his/her description, you would have an accurate understanding of the truth regarding zero gravity. However, if we assume you boarded the next space shuttle and took a ride to space, the truth you learned from the astronaut has now become validated by personal experience. The experience of having flown in a space vehicle beyond the earth's atmosphere has corroborated the knowledge you were given by the astronaut and solidified that truth in you. In the same way, when we live life with knowledge of the truth, every day the truth becomes validated through experiences. The result is our understanding of the truth grows deeper and stronger. Furthermore, knowing the truth benefits us each day of life, if we use the truth. As we continue to live our lives in harmony with the truth, our lives are enriched, ultimately leading to unrestrained joy! The intent of this book is to not only clarify the key concepts of truth, God, and love, but to demonstrate how a person's life can be positively affected by applying the understanding of these concepts to everyday life.

The title of this book reflects the goal of this book, which is to remove distorted perspectives of the truth. The clarification of the truth means certain aspects of truth that were not known now become known. In fact, as the truth becomes clearer, there are a couple of significant connections that become apparent. Truth, God, and love are not only related, but are equivalent. As we explore the concepts presented in this book, evidence of the equivalency of truth, God, and love surfaces. Hence, the subtitle God=Love=Truth. The cover of this book presents the subtitle in circular form designed specifically to illustrate the equivalent nature of these terms. The colors chosen also have meaning. Gold was chosen for the word God. Gold represents the Godhead. Gold also is associated with other things such as wealth and prosperity, however, the Godhead is the relevant meaning in this case. Orange was chosen for the word love. Most people think of red when thinking of the color of love. However, the love we focus on in this book is Agape love. Agape love is God's love. God's love is the most powerful form of love. When we are conduits of Agape love, we experience much joy. Joy and enthusiasm are associated with the color orange, as is intensity of emotion. Therefore, because the intensity of the emotion of joy is felt when Agape love flows through us, the color orange was selected for the word love. Blue was chosen for the word truth. Blue symbolizes truth, but also symbolizes trust, loyalty, wisdom, faith, and heaven. The colors chosen to represent the words God, love, and truth on the cover of this book were not random, but, please know that mankind's association of certain colors with specific characteristics, emotions, or a variety of other nouns is somewhat arbitrary. In fact, there are many meanings that vary from culture to culture across the earth.

I want to acknowledge my wife, Melissa, regarding her contributions in helping clarify truth. Melissa and I had numerous conversations over the course of approximately one year regarding various topics that are addressed in this book. It is important to obtain the opinions of others as you seek the truth. Melissa's opinions have been invaluable to me for several reasons. Most importantly, she is connected to God through Jesus Christ. She is also my wife and we have certainly become one. That does not mean we are identical people, but it does mean the Holy Spirit has joined us together in the spiritual dimension. This happens through supernatural intervention by God (a subject addressed throughout the book and covered in depth in chapter 12). You certainly improve your understanding of the truth when you discuss the truth with someone who is also pursuing an understanding of the truth. And, although you can do this with anyone who is pursuing the truth, and you should, there is no better person to share deep spiritual truths with than the person with whom you have become one. Extremely effective communication exists between two people whose souls have been knit together. There is also enhanced communication because of the amount of time spent communicating with each other in general as life is lived together.

There are a couple of essential thoughts to keep in mind as you wander through the pages of this book. First, there cannot be more than one truth about a given subject. There is only truth and untruth. For example, we cannot know for certain whether or not there is physical life in the universe outside of ours on earth. Let's assume there is no physical life outside of planet earth. One person believes there is life outside of humans on planet earth somewhere in the universe. Another person believes that the only life to be found in the universe is what exists on planet earth. One of these people is right while the other is wrong. Believing in something other than the truth does not change the truth, or make the truth any less valid. It does mean the person who believes an untruth has not learned about or recognized the truth yet. Let's consider another example. I was working outside in the backyard recently and was stung by a wasp. Subsequent to being stung, I shared what had happened to me with Melissa. She could choose to doubt that I was stung. If so, the fact that Melissa chooses to believe I wasn't stung by a wasp does not alter in any way the fact that I was stung. What it does mean is Melissa does not believe the truth.

The second thought to keep in mind as you read this book is fundamental truths are best understood when we think about what they really mean. This may sound like a very simplistic statement, however, many people fail to understand a truth because they do not put enough effort into understanding what the truth really means. Often, you just need to ask a few questions and the truth surfaces. So, be ready to dig deep, to put effort into understanding the truths that are presented, and attempt to see and comprehend the truths without preconceived biases.

Our sincere hope is that bringing clarity to truth will accomplish several things. A brief discussion of these potential accomplishments follows organized by the type of person receiving the clarity.

For the person who believes Jesus Christ is God, the clarity will generate a flood of enthusiasm for the God they already recognize. Often, believers in Jesus Christ will acknowledge who He is in terms of being their God, but fail to fully realize the magnitude of whom they are talking about. The lack of realization of who God is also inhibits the accurate thinking regarding who we are. Once the realization of who God is occurs, we begin to understand how insignificant we are when compared to God. This is not self-defeating thinking. On the contrary, it is the comprehension of who we are versus who God is that leads one to conclude how fortunate we are to be loved so deeply by our great God! That is an encouraging and motivating thought. In addition, understanding the truth about God more clearly leads us to enhancing our relationship with Him, which is the ultimate pathway to empowerment in our life now and forever.

The second type of person we can identify is someone who does not believe Jesus Christ is God, but does believe there is a God. For these folks, the facts they have absorbed about the world and life during their own existence have created a worldview that concludes there must be someone bigger than themselves. Furthermore, they typically believe that the "someone bigger than themselves" created all that is seen, including human life. Understanding the wisdom and knowledge God offers us will not only validate for these individuals their own thinking that there is a God, but provide deeper insight into who He is. The additional insight is something to be treasured and sought after by those who believe there is a God. Our hope is this appetite to know more and comprehend more fully who God is will keep the minds of those who believe there is a God open to receive the truth and accept it when enough evidence is presented. And, if that intellectual bridge is crossed, the new enlightenment will be the impetus for internal energy to be directed toward a more focused pursuit of the true God as well as all that He has to offer us, and what He expects of us, as we experience a direct, deep relationship with Him.

The last group we want to define are those who are unconvinced that God exists. Clarifying truth about who God is will be met with a reluctance to accept what is communicated due to a preconceived notion, and sometimes strongly held belief, that opposes the truth. Although some may think that people in this group would have the most difficult time modifying their worldview based upon receiving clarification of truth, the power of God's truths should never be underestimated. Some would even go so far as to cite John, chapter 8, the scripture beginning at verse 42 through the end of the chapter, as a reason that those who do not believe the truth will not be able to hear it. In this passage, Jesus is telling His audience that they are unable to hear what He says because they are not of God, they are essentially of the world, or worse yet, of Satan. However, we all started out as unrepentant sinners, separated from God, yet many have had their spiritual blinders removed by the power of God's Word, which is the truth and is God Himself. This phenomenon applies to every person who knows the truth, accepts the truth, and lives in accordance with the truth.

During your life, you may have heard something that you reacted to as a new revelation. As we live our lives, we grow in our understanding of truth, which results in gained wisdom. We obtain clarity of many things. There are literally millions of examples. These range from simple truths related to fables or stories such as when we come to the realization that there is no tooth fairy to more complex truths such as trees give off oxygen and take in carbon dioxide while human bodies do just the opposite. Any truth is good for us to understand. The understanding of truth is essentially obtaining knowledge about reality. This comprehension of reality is a stabilizing force in our lives, i.e., something we can count on as a basis for living a successful life. In other words, knowledge of reality serves to provide an intellectual foundation that we will use each day.

Many things may interfere with our ability to understand deep truths. One example is the pace of life. Many people are so busy earning a living or raising their children that tackling the more difficult subjects such as who God is and who we are in relation to Him are not at the top of our priority list due to competing priorities that require our attention. Regardless of whether or not a person takes the time to understand spiritual truths, those truths exist, and are explainable. Every truth exists whether or not we are aware of it or whether or not we believe it. For example, a physics truth is that gravity exists. The force of gravity is measured by the acceleration of falling objects. We cannot see gravity, but we can see the effects of gravity. If a person does not believe gravity is real, there is little consequence in their life unless they put themselves in danger by walking off a cliff or tall building thinking that they will not fall. In these cases, the consequences of not believing the truth could be lethal for the person's physical body. It is not important to understand precisely how gravity works, but that it exists and what precautions should be followed to ensure gravity works for our benefit rather than being exposed to circumstances where the force of gravity could harm us.

Similar to the gravity example, we do not have to understand precisely how a spiritual truth works, but know that the spiritual truth exists, understand what it means, and how we can apply the spiritual truth to our lives. We receive the benefits of the spiritual truth and protection from negative consequences when we abide by a spiritual truth.

Melissa and I hope that this book will help you by delivering truth with clarity in a concise manner. We also hope that a deeper comprehension of God and His truths will, for many, be life changing.

CHAPTER 1

What Affects Our Belief/Unbelief in God?

The accurate view of God and the multitude of misperceptions of God are attributable to a number of factors. The largest factor is a person's worldview, which is formed from the accumulated experiences in life including what is learned from significant influencers in the person's life. Those influencers include parents, grandparents, and other extended family members who are typically older than the person whose life they are influencing. In addition, influencers include teachers, coaches, public figures, and authors of anything written or spoken that a person reads or listens to from any text or media source. A person's own experiences are also a very significant influencer. For example, if, at an early age, a person touches a hot stovetop and burns him/herself, the thought of that experience reaches a place in the person's mind that very clearly becomes a strong force in terms of guiding or shaping future behavior. The probability that the person who burned their hand will repeat the action that led to the burned hand is very low. Another example of an experience that will have a significant influence on future behavior is the death of someone close to you. There are very few people who go through life, unless their own amount of time on earth is short, without experiencing a loss through the passing on of someone they love. It is one of those experiences that you never forget, whether you were in the room with the person who died at the time of their passing or heard of the news via a phone call or some other form of electronic communication. You will forever remember exactly where you were at the moment the traumatic event occurred, whether present or distant from the event itself. How the death of a loved one affects our future behavior depends on the relationship we had with the departed. If a person was not on good terms with the departed, there may be feelings of regret. If the departed had hurt us in some way, there may finally be closure on a painful part of our past. If the departed was the person we loved more than any other person in our life, the sadness will initially be overwhelming. In addition, the grief will be paralyzing mentally and spiritually. The intense feelings can even lead to depression. The intensity of the feelings will obviously have a significant impact on future behavior of the person who suffered the loss. Typically, the pain of the loss will subside over time, however, the event will never cease to be an influencer of future behavior for many reasons. If, for example, the loss was a grandfather whom had enormous positive influence in a person's life including mentoring and teaching important core values, there would naturally be a sense that a person who lost their grandfather would be grateful for that mentoring. Furthermore, the gratefulness may guide future behavior inasmuch as a person may be motivated to conduct their lives as to make the departed proud. It is not unusual that a person would want the departed, if they were still on earth, to say, "I'm so proud of you." How does this relate to our perception of who God is? If the departed had a strong faith in God, expressed or demonstrated their faith through their actions to the person who was mentored/

loved, the person who suffered the loss would tend to have a view of God highly influenced by the departed person. Interestingly, you can conclude that if the departed was an atheist, the lack of belief in God would also influence the person who was mentored/loved. Therefore, it is easy to see the influence one person can have on another. Some of those influences we carry with us for the rest of our lives.

On the other hand, there are experiences that are painful or negative in some way, but have very limited influence on future behavior or result in a permanent change in thinking. For example, if a person receives a speeding ticket, they will likely slow down for the rest of the day, and be more cautious for a short period of time. However, in many cases, the reasons for speeding in the first place (running late or impatience or a general habit of desiring to be somewhere sooner rather than later) will tend to overtake the memory of receiving the speeding ticket in terms of influencing future behavior. So, the experience of receiving a speeding ticket is real, and will influence future behavior, but the amount of influence that experience has on future behavior will diminish with the passage of time. Another example is the common, and often painful, experience of the loss of a pet. Even though some people are as close to a pet as some of their closest relatives, and the loss could be traumatic emotionally, there is typically little that the pet did to shape a person's worldview and influence future behavior in terms of a belief system. At most, adopting and caring for a pet may reinforce the fact that animals were created, just as we have been created. That is not to ignore the fact that a true, deep emotional bond between a person and their pet is real and rooted in love. As evidence of the emotions directly related to, and subsequent to, the loss of a pet, we often observe people acquiring a new pet to help soothe the grief and other emotions associated with the loss.

Each day we live on earth we are subjected to new experiences and new interactions with influencers in our life which result in a constantly changing worldview. At times the change comes in the form of a dramatic shift due to a strong experience or a significant enlightenment received from an influencer in our life while other changes to our worldview are subtle and very gradual. The latter change can be characterized as a minor modification to a deeply held belief. If you reflect upon your life, it is easy to see how your worldview has changed over time. You can engage in this self-reflection regardless of your current age. In other words, you are never too young for self-reflection. For example, a thirty-five year old individual can remember some of their thinking as a teenager. The change in thinking during the time period since the thirty-five year old was a teenager, which is, hopefully, significant, can be largely due to learning more about the world and/or God during the time lived since the teen years.

The process of constantly evolving thought is something that can and should be recognized and embraced while it is occurring. Many people allow the process to occur naturally and sometimes with a sense of randomness (as if they are not even cognizant of it), while others put forth focused effort on expanding their thought horizon and seek diligently to know more truth. The thinking of the former folks will tend to be less of an intentional pursuit of knowledge, as if the growing repository of learnings is something that just happens to them. The driving force of the changing thought for these thinkers are the day to day things that occur in their lives, usually experiences on the job, interactions within relationships with others, and the most common experiences that most people face. These include activities such as going to visit a doctor, or a stop at your bank, or a shopping excursion. On the other hand, the group of people described above who actively seek truth have a deep rooted passion to know more and, most importantly, know more truth. They are not unaffected by the activities that we described as having a significant impact on the evolution of thought of the former group of people. However, their passion to learn more truth will lead them to focus their efforts more intensely on learning. As they carry this learning mode mindset with them throughout each day, the more mundane parts of life, such as going to work every day in a job with much repetition or visiting the department of motor vehicles to obtain a new driver's license, will have less impact on the thought process evolution of these individuals as compared to reading the Bible or other philosophical and theological material. These thinkers seem to be more interested in attempting to gain insight into deep spiritual truths.

Whether or not a person's focus is to learn more truth will affect how a person approaches everything in which an individual participates regardless of the task. In other words, having a desire to accumulate truth will be a driving force within the person perpetually. Lack of this desire will lead to a thought process evolution that can be characterized by a more passive approach to learning.

For those who desire to learn continually, there is another very important distinction that should be highlighted. It is much easier for the person who seeks truth in an honest manner, without deeply held preconceived thoughts that will act as a bias, to find the truth than for a person who seeks truth but holds a worldview that includes some untruths that have been accepted as truth.

It is more difficult for a person who doesn't seek truth or have a subconscious goal of learning each day to stumble upon deep spiritual truths because the learning would be inadvertent. The most successful way of expanding your knowledge bank of truth is to have a determination associated with each day of life to want more truth. This determination is fueled by understanding that truth is not only helpful in terms of leading to a more productive life, but essential to opening the doors of wisdom.

Another point of clarity needed is to ensure full awareness of what wisdom and knowledge are and how the desire to gain an understanding of truth is related to each. Wisdom and knowledge are different, but there is an interesting interdependence. Knowledge is obtaining a clear understanding of something. Wisdom is putting that understanding to work in decision-making that will impact your life, and potentially others' lives. As noted earlier, knowledge gained can be based in truth or untruth. If the knowledge you learn is truth, the wisdom used in your life will impact your life, and others you interact with, in a positive way. If the knowledge you learn is untruth, the wisdom used in your life will impact your life, and others you interact with, in a negative way. For example, if we gain a substantial amount of knowledge about the chemistry of our physical bodies, that knowledge can lead to wisdom used to maximize our health. If that knowledge is based upon truth, and in wisdom we act upon that knowledge, we will experience positive impacts to our health. If the knowledge gained about the chemistry of the body is rooted in untruth, and we act upon that knowledge, we will not experience the positive impacts to our health that we expected. So, the overarching principle here is that gaining knowledge rooted in truth and having that understanding of truth shape your worldview (how you see life) will lead to positive changes to your life. The converse is also true. Gaining knowledge rooted in untruth and having that understanding of untruth shape your worldview will lead to negative changes to your life. Hence, the goal of every human being should be to seek to understand truth regardless of the subject. The accumulation of truth will always result in something positive in a person's life.

The foundational principle we just discussed can be extrapolated into the spiritual dimension. If there are spiritual truths that are not obvious without putting forth significant effort to find them, the people who do not focus on seeking truth as a standard practice in their life would tend to not gain knowledge of these spiritual truths. However, those who seek truth as they live each day would have a much better chance at finding spiritual truths, although finding these spiritual truths is clearly not an outcome that is guaranteed because spiritual untruths are just as prevalent as spiritual truths.

Let's convert this principle into a practical summary. If there is a God, there will be people who come to know Him as they pursue spiritual truths because they will find truth during their pursuit. If there is a God, there will also be people who either deny His existence or misinterpret who He is because, during their pursuit of spiritual truths, they have come to accept as a spiritual truth one or more spiritual untruths. The latter group of individuals may have just as much desire to find and understand truth as the former group of individuals, but have unfortunately found untruth, and believe untruth. Furthermore, if there is a God, there will be great benefits associated with finding the spiritual truth about Him. Conversely, if there is a God, there will be devastating consequences if what a person believes are spiritual truths are untrue. Lastly, the group of individuals who do not intentionally pursue understanding of spiritual truths will likely not find them, whether or not untruths are part of their belief system.

Everything discussed to this point is intended to be the basis for having a framework in our minds that can be used to understand why people misperceive who God is and the thought process that takes place leading to a misperception. If what has been presented so far in this chapter were all there was to the phenomenon of either understanding who God is or not, you might conclude that understanding who God is may be based upon a fortunate set of circumstances that led a person who pursued spiritual truth to find it or aspects of it and an unfortunate set of circumstances that led a person who pursued spiritual truth to not find it. A similar conclusion could be reached for those who do not pursue knowledge or spiritual truth. However, these hypothetical conclusions are inaccurate. Human comprehension of truth is not predicated on random circumstances, but rather the intentional discovery and understanding of spiritual matters. That does not mean God does not work through circumstances in our lives to teach us and strengthen us. It does mean that every human being has the opportunity to seek truth and find truth, regardless of circumstances in their life. The fact that many people do not find the truth is evidence that something is interfering with the process of seeing truth clearly. To understand what causes the interference we must acquire some knowledge about the spiritual dimension. There are forces at work in the spiritual dimension that need to be explained. These forces are God (which we refer to as God the Father, Jesus Christ, and the Holy Spirit), God's angels, and the enemies of God (which we refer to as Satan and his demons). The next chapter will be devoted to a thorough discussion of these forces that affect each one of us.

CHAPTER 2

Spiritual Forces

For those who do not believe God exists or that Jesus Christ is God, we are asking you to, for a moment, assume there is a God and the Word of God (the Bible) is His communication to us for our benefit. For reference, throughout this book, when the Bible is quoted, we are using the New International Version (NIV) of the Bible. In the Word of God, we are often told of an ongoing battle in the spiritual dimension. This battle has no boundaries in terms of where it takes place. Every human being is involved in the battle, whether they know it or not. This battle is between the forces of good and evil. God leads the forces of good and Satan leads the forces of evil. The opposing forces have desired outcomes that are in conflict. Satan and his demons attempt to distract us from God's truth, entice us to commit sin inasmuch as sin separates us from God, and seek to destroy us (the book of John, chapter 10, verse 10, "The thief comes only to steal and kill and destroy" and the book of

1 Peter, chapter 5, verse 8, "Be alert and of sober mind. Your enemy the devil prowls around like a roaring lion looking for someone to devour." The most serious destruction referred to in these scriptures is spiritual death, or equivalently and more clearly, eternal separation from God. In delineating between physical and spiritual death, God is telling us not to fear physical death, because if you know Him and live for Him during your life on earth, you will live eternally with Him after your physical body expires. The "eternity with God" outcome is not only everlasting but an experience filled with constant joy and should be what we focus on in our lives that drives our behavior. We will discuss life after death much more thoroughly later in this book.

How much do we know about the forces of good and evil? The average person may not know much about these forces, or may underestimate the power these forces possess. However, God gives us the ability to gain much knowledge about these forces through what He has already communicated to us. The words Satan, demon, demons, demon possessed, or evil are mentioned 205 times in the Bible. The words good, holy, angel, or angels are mentioned 1,547 times in the Bible. If a person were to read each sentence in the Bible that contains one of these words, that person would gain a deep understanding of the spiritual dimension. God emphatically strives to teach us about the spiritual dimension, but many people fail to acknowledge that it even exists. Individuals whom do not acknowledge that the spiritual dimension exists may express statements such as, "This physical life is all there is and when I die, that is the end." That perspective is precisely what our spiritual enemy (Satan) would like us all to possess. If a person truly believed that what we see physically is all there is, there would be no reason to consider what happens when the physical body dies. Furthermore, without the curiosity of life after death (discussion in chapter 11), a person is more likely to conduct their life on earth with a bent toward selfish desires. Why? Two reasons. First, the person does not have God in their life to serve so they serve themselves through self-indulgence. Second, without God the human existence has an emptiness. In the book of Job, chapter 15, verses 31-35, Eliphaz, one of Job's counselors, tells Job, "Let him not deceive himself by trusting what is worthless, for he will get nothing in return. Before his time he will wither, and his branches will not flourish. He will be like a vine stripped of its unripe grapes, like an olive tree shedding its blossoms. For the company of the godless will be barren, and fire will consume the tents of those who love bribes. They conceive trouble and give birth to evil; their womb fashions deceit." This passage of scripture is describing some of the consequences of living a life without God. A life without God is an unfulfilled life because there is no fruit produced. Fruit that is produced in our lives (which God talks about in scripture) is produced when we love others. We will dig more into this in chapter 8.

The pursuit of selfish desires inevitably leads to sin. This has been true from the beginning (please read the account of Adam and Eve, the book of Genesis, chapters 2 and 3). The pursuit of selfish desires has been a struggle throughout the existence of humanity. In the book of Romans, chapter 7, verse 19, God cites through the Apostle Paul this fact, "For I do not do the good I want to do, but the evil I do not want to do, this I keep on doing." It is essential to recognize that every person is immersed in a spiritual battle. Without this recognition, a person is unable to fight. It is virtually impossible for a person to defeat something that they do not know exists. An army battalion can be given the most powerful weapons, but if they do not know who the enemy is, the tactics and goals of the enemy, and understand what they are fighting for, they will fail to be victorious (i.e. defeat the enemy). As we live our lives entrenched in this constant and unavoidable spiritual battle between the forces of good and evil, please do not think for a moment we are helpless. God has given us the ability to choose good and not evil. How unfair would it be for God to say, "I have this amazing gift for you....eternal life with me....but you need to defeat evil in your life while on earth. Good luck. You're on your own." He did not say that nor leaves us unprepared for the battle. In fact, He has given us what we need to defeat the enemy, but we must act upon the instructions He has provided. In the book of Ephesians, chapter 6, verses 10-17, God talks about the spiritual battle and what we can do to protect ourselves and defeat the enemy. He says, "Finally, be strong in the LORD and in his mighty power. Put on the full armor of God, so that you can take your stand against the devil's schemes. For our struggle is not against flesh and blood, but against the rulers, against the authorities, against the powers of this dark world and against the spiritual forces of evil in the heavenly realms. Therefore put on the full armor of God, so that when the day of evil comes, you may be able to stand your ground, and after you have done everything, to stand. Stand firm then, with the belt of truth buckled around your waist, with the breastplate of righteousness in place, and with your feet fitted with the readiness that comes from the gospel of peace. In addition to all this, take up the shield of faith, with which you can extinguish all the flaming arrows of the evil one. Take the helmet of salvation and the sword of the Spirit, which is the word of God." There is much in this passage of scripture, but we want to highlight just a couple of key points.

First, God is very clearly describing the battle as a spiritual battle, but nonetheless, very real battle. Do not be misled by the words, "spiritual forces of evil in heavenly realms" into thinking that the spiritual forces of evil exist in Heaven. The "heavenly" realm described here is equivalent to the "spiritual" realm. God is teaching us that there are powers at work against us in this world (on earth), and, at the same time, are unseen because they exist in the spiritual dimension. Secondly, the devil intentionally plans his attacks on us. These are referred to in the scripture as schemes. Why would Satan attack us? Always remember Satan hates God, and us. And his ultimate goal is to separate us from God forever, which is the opposite of what God wants. Thirdly, if we are prepared and put the whole armor on, we will be able to stand our ground and defeat the enemy. The pieces of armor are designed to protect us. Truth, righteousness, the gospel of peace, faith, and salvation are the elements. As discussed at length in chapter 1, truth is vitally important and something we all should attempt to understand. Righteousness is living according to and in obedience of God's commands. The gospel of peace is our source of readiness. Understanding who God is, that Jesus Christ is God, and that we will fight for what we know makes us ready for the fight. The importance of steadfast faith cannot be overstated. Faith is likened to a shield in this passage of scripture, which is able to block the attacks from the enemy. If doubt ever enters our minds, we must refresh our minds with the facts and continuously communicate with God to remain strong. Salvation is also a vital piece of the armor. God offers salvation to us as a free gift. We must take the knowledge we gain about Him, draw conclusions about the great spiritual truths, and accept His free gift to us to attain salvation. Accepting His gift is simultaneously turning from sin because we learned that sin separates us from God, whereas when we accept His gift we become united with God. Lastly, there is one piece of armor that is not defensive, but offensive. The sword of the Spirit, which God calls the His word, is intended for us to defeat the enemy, rather than just protect ourselves. If we read and understand God's word, we will have a powerful tool that will be used to defeat the enemy. When the enemy tempts us and lies to us, we will know what God said and expose Satan's lies, rendering the lies powerless against us. Doing this in everyday life is not as difficult as many think, but it does take effort.

Let's discuss a couple of examples of how we can be tempted and how we can defeat the enemy. God tells us not to steal in the books of Exodus, chapter 20, Leviticus, chapter 19, Deuteronomy, chapter 5, Matthew, chapter 19, Mark, chapter 10, and Luke, chapter 18. Satan will tempt some by telling us that it is not a big deal to adjust our income tax return in effect to increase a refund or reduce an amount owed to the federal government. The lie may continue by the notion that the government taxes people too much and has plenty so it is somehow justification for individuals to receive more or pay less. However, falsifying your tax return is stealing, which God forbids, and also a crime in the secular world. In the book of Matthew, chapter 22, and Mark, chapter 12, and Luke, chapter 20, God is telling us to pay our taxes and pay what is due. If we know what scripture, God's word, says about stealing and about paying taxes, we can use that scripture to defeat the enemy....in this case that means pay our taxes fully. When we pay our taxes fully, we avoid sin and separation from God. When we avoid sin, we are also essentially telling Satan to leave us alone because what he attempted failed. Another form of stealing from the government is avoiding paying taxes by taking money "under the table" and not reporting some bona fide income. Similar to previous example, the consequences or benefits of actions taken are identical to the first example.

The sins we have just discussed are two-fold....stealing *and* lying. A few examples of God telling us not to lie can be found in the books of Exodus, chapter 23, Leviticus, chapter 19, and Proverbs, chapter's 6, 12, and 19. Lying can damage relationships in as much as healthy relationships are built on trust. Lying is sin and separates us from God. Lying often accompanies other types of sin. However, if we equip ourselves with the armor we discussed and the sword, or God's word, we can protect ourselves and defeat the enemy.

Another example of temptation from the enemy is lust. In our current culture in America, lust is not only seldom thought of as sin, but often engaged in unashamedly and even boastfully. Adultery, for many, holds the same status in terms of not being ashamed and even being boastful. As a side note, our culture promotes provocative or non-modest attire designed to attract the opposite gender, or in some cases, the same gender. In the book of Matthew, chapter 5, God says, "that anyone who looks at a woman lustfully has already committed adultery with her in his heart." Of course, this also applies to women who look at a man lustfully, or any gender looking at any gender lustfully. Again, if we are armed with God's word, we are equipped to defeat the enemy when the initial temptation arrives.

This leads us to another bit of instruction from God. In the book of 2 Corinthians, chapter 10, verse 5 God tells us to, "take every thought captive." What this means is when a sinful temptation from Satan enters our mind, we are to stop it before we act upon the initial thought. If God tells us to take every thought captive, you can be certain He gives us the ability to do so. Filling our minds with wisdom from God, putting on our armor, and recognizing immediately the attacks from Satan enable us to take every thought captive. We will discuss this further in subsequent chapters of this book. Without equipping ourselves, we become defenseless.

Adam and Eve appeared to be defenseless to the temptations. We should ask ourselves why this was the case. This couple, whom lived in a utopian place, had direct fellowship with God, and had wonderful provision, was somehow not content when offered more. They were tempted by Satan, whom they did not realize hated God and whose goal was to separate them from God. How were Adam and Eve deceived? Satan lied and appealed to Adam and Eve's selfish desires. In this case, offering them the ability to be like God by gaining wisdom through partaking in the fruit of the tree of the knowledge of good and evil. What Adam and Eve were told by Satan was obviously a lie, but Adam and Eve's selfish desires kept them ignorant of the fact that they were becoming the victims of a lie. A lie that they acted upon, and that action initiated the separation from God. They did precisely what God asked them not to do. Disobedience to what God asks of us is sin. The ramifications of sin for Adam and Eve were not just unpleasant (death became a reality, perfect harmony within all of creation ceased, and they were banished from the Garden of Eden), but changed their entire future existence and relationship with God.

The root of every sin is selfishness. God has provided a clear definition of sin by giving us many examples of people who sinned and by defining the opposite of sin, which is holiness. In fact, we often see examples of people who demonstrate the existence of holiness and sin in their behavior. One powerful example is David. In the book of 1 Samuel, chapter 13, verse 14 and the book of Acts, chapter 13, verse 22, God called David a man after God's own heart. Desiring holiness in your life, which would be the tangible evidence of a person who wants a heart like God's, was certainly an attribute of David. At the same time, he had to repent for the sin that took place in his life, which included adultery and orchestrating a murder. You can see from this one example that the impact of the spiritual forces of good and evil are powerful, real, and can cause any person to love and obey God as well as sin and disobey God.

Sin is succumbing to temptation by acting upon the thoughts that cross our mind that are not holy or motivated by love. Another way to describe sin is fulfilling selfish desires. Anger is a sin. If we become angry and lose our patience with another person, we are thinking more about ourselves than the person we become angry with. The manifestation of anger in our behavior is clearly the result of only looking at ourselves. For example, if you are driving in heavy traffic and a person in a vehicle from behind us takes a path around you and squeezes in the line of traffic in front of you, this act by the other driver could cause an angry reaction within you. The other driver may not have been driving in a courteous manner, but if our reaction to the other driver's behavior is anger, we have sinned. The root cause of the sin is the feeling that the other driver did something unfair to us. That root cause is based upon thinking of ourselves. Another example of sin is if you are in a social setting with friends and someone in the group is sharing about events in their life that indicated a certain sense of accomplishment. You may feel compelled to discuss events in your life that show a similar accomplishment, and may exaggerate or completely make up the events in your life. That, of course, is lying, because part of what we say is untrue. Why did we feel compelled to lie? Because we wanted to be liked, or accepted, or admired by the group. However, the exact opposite will occur if folks see through the lie. We need to dwell upon who we are and be content with who we are. We do not need to embellish anything about our lives to impress others or be accepted by others. All we really need to do is love others. That subject will be explored deeply in the next chapter of this book.

Our human nature, apart from God, is drawn toward sin because our natural way of thinking is to consider our own needs and desires before others. That is a struggle for every human being, but a struggle that can be overcome. How do we overcome self-centered thinking and, therefore, defeat sin? By engaging in the power of love.

CHAPTER 3

The Winning Power – God's Love

This is likely the most important chapter in this book. When we gain an understanding of the power of God's love and how to tap into it, only good transpires as we use it. In addition, we experience more of who God really is because we have the power of His love at work within us. For clarification of this concept, let's assume you have been educated on the health benefits of drinking orange juice. We are told by some in the medical community and nutritional health professionals that the vitamin C content in orange juice gives it antioxidant benefits, which, if consumed, helps our body's immune system defend itself from sickness or recover from minor sickness more quickly. In addition, the potassium content in orange juice helps regulate fluid balance in our bodies and helps our muscles operate effectively. Many people think orange juice tastes delicious, although some prefer pulp and some do not. Let's assume you have an unlimited supply of orange juice. Let's also assume you cannot obtain the health benefits of drinking orange juice from any other source. If you never drink orange juice you will never realize the benefits associated with orange juice, whether you are aware of those benefits or not. Likewise with God's love. Some people do not tap into the power of God's love and, therefore, cannot obtain the benefits of His love working in and through them. What prevents folks from tapping into God's love? Some people do not tap into God's love because they deny the existence of God, or in their minds cannot prove nor disprove the existence of God, rendering His power in their life unachievable. Some people do not tap into God's love because, although they believe in God, they do not fully understand how to tap into His love. Before exploring all the benefits of God's love working in and through us, and how to tap into His love, we must first fully comprehend what God's love is and how it differs from other types of love.

In the books of Deuteronomy, chapter 6, verse 5, Matthew, chapter 22, verse 37, Mark, chapter 12, verse 30, and Luke, chapter 10, verse 27 God tells us to "Love the Lord your God with all your heart, all your soul (mind), and all your strength." In the books of Matthew, Mark, and Luke, God goes on to add "Love your neighbor as yourself." When we love someone, we are certainly not being selfish. To thoroughly understand this, we must first define what loving someone means. It is not difficult to determine whether or not you love someone if you apply God's standard to love. God's love is not lusting because of a person's physical appearance. Physical love is called Eros. Neither of God's commands to love cited above involve physical appearance. We are expected to love God whom we cannot see physically. We are expected to love others as much as we love ourselves. Loving yourself is loving **who you are**, not **what you look like**. In the same manner, the love God commands us to have for another is loving who they are, not what they look like. God's love is also not brotherly, or friendship love. This type of love is called Philia love. Philia love is liking another person for a specific attribute, for example, a great sense of humor. God's love is much deeper and enables us to live in a completely unselfish manner as we focus entirely on what is good for another person in all circumstances. God's love is called Agape love, because it comes from Him, and is who He is. What is most thrilling is that we get to demonstrate and experience Agape love toward God and others because He gives us the ability to do so. This ability is only possible by loving Him and when we do, the indwelling of His Holy Spirit is accomplished in us. With God's Holy Spirit within us, we are empowered to love God and others with His love, Agape love. This empowerment to love God and others with Agape love is something we can only experience if we strive each day to have a relationship with God. Many have only a superficial knowledge of, and relationship to, the true God. It is as if some folks are walking through life with an acknowledgment of God so that they have a spiritual safety net for what may happen after their time on earth is over. In other words, in the mind of a person who has only a superficial relationship with God, if they profess belief in God, there will be a pleasant outcome once their physical body passes away. Unfortunately, the truth is that many will stand before God and expect to enter heaven and not be permitted to enter. The reason is during their life on earth they did not truly do what God asked. In the book of Matthew, chapter 7, verses 21-23 God tells us that "not everyone who says to me, Lord, Lord, will enter the kingdom of heaven." He does tell us exactly who will enter the kingdom of heaven. "Those who do the will of the Father, who is in heaven." So, what is God's will? We devote an entire chapter to God's will in this book, chapter 8. But, for purposes of our current discussion, God's will for us are His commands to us. He commanded us to love the Lord your God with all your heart, all your soul, and all your mind and to love your neighbor as yourself. He also commanded us to obey His commandments provided to Moses in Deuteronomy, chapter 5. Every person can obey God's commandments as long as he/she has the Holy Spirit within him/her. How do we receive the Holy Spirit? By repenting of our sins and turning away from any unbelief in our soul. When we do that, we begin to live for God. We desire to know more of Him. We diligently seek to understand His Word. If you are reading this, you are seeking to understand truth, which is His Word. This desire to know more of Him, if acted upon, will lead to a deeper relationship with Him. The deeper relationship with Him leads to the use of God's love in our lives. This means that our spiritual being gains a closeness to God not experienced before the Holy Spirit came to empower us.

So, please do not make the mistake of believing that acknowledgement of God is all that is needed to guarantee a passageway to heaven. Heaven, as our eternal destination, can be attained by being fully dedicated to obeying God and desiring to know more of Him. As we do this, we become sanctified through the deeper understanding of His holiness. This deeper understanding permeates our being to the extent that we begin to reflect, by our actions, a more righteous, or holy, life. Sanctification is a process, not an event. In the book of John, chapter 17, verse 17, God shows us that we are sanctified by the truth and that His Word is truth. As we experience more of God's love in us, and as we learn more about Him by exploring His Word, and as we do His will, our thoughts and actions become those of holiness rather than sinfulness. That is not to say that we could ever lead a sinless existence. We will always struggle with our sin nature. There is no better description of this struggle than in the book of Romans, chapter 7, verses 15-20. Verse 19 was cited earlier, but the full passage referenced here will provide deeper insight into the description of our struggle.

It is impossible to love with Agape love and not move toward holiness in your life. Or, for those of you who dislike double negatives, as you love with Agape love it is inevitable that you move toward holiness. There is no difference between Agape love and holiness. Both terms are the nature of God. As we love others with Agape love and move toward holiness in our lives, our struggle with sin diminishes, but never to the point that the struggle is entirely overcome. We never dispense with our sin nature. It is always a part of us. We can, however, have many successes every day as holy thoughts and actions replace unholy thoughts and actions. The more we love, the less we sin. The more we love, the less we dwell on unholy things.

It is important to note that God does not put a limit on how much we can or should love others. The reason is He has no limits on His love for us and defines that phenomenon or condition as perfect love. He also tells us that the greatest love we can demonstrate for another is to die for them. He did. If you are willing to die for someone, how can you not love them? For most of us, it is not hard to think of a person in our lives for whom we would die. For example, let's assume you are with your young son, daughter, grandson, granddaughter, sister, brother, nephew, or niece and you are crossing a street. As you are crossing the street, a speeding car turns onto the same street and is heading directly toward the young child in your life. There is only enough time to throw yourself in front of the speeding vehicle and push the child out of danger, however, that action will likely result in serious injury or even death to yourself. Making the split second decision to go ahead with that action without regard to the physical consequences of your behavior, clearly means you love the child with the greatest love, or Agape love. The book of John, chapter 15, verse 13 sum this love best, "Greater love has no one than this: to lay down one's life for one's friends."

Agape love is defined in the book of 1 Corinthians, chapter 13, verses 4-8. That scripture reads as follows, "Love is patient, love is kind. It does not envy, it does not boast, it is not proud. It does not dishonor others, it is not self-seeking, it is not easily angered, it keeps no record of wrongs. Love does not delight in evil but rejoices with the truth. It always protects, always trusts, always hopes, always perseveres. Love never fails." Every word in that passage portrays the person doing the loving as having a complete focus on the person whom he/she loves and not thinking of themselves. If you love a person as God loves you (perfectly) there is nothing you would not do for the person you love. The ability to love perfectly does not come naturally because our sin nature, as discussed previously, makes us lean or gravitate toward selfishness.

Imagine if you were to live each day with the ability to exercise love at all times to all people. You certainly would never have a bad day! And, you would rarely think about what is best for yourself because you would constantly be loving others. We can even conclude that you would be in a perpetually unselfish state. Remember what love is defined as. Always patient, kind, etc. We shall focus on love's first attribute, patience, for a moment. When we are patient with someone, we are being unselfish. We are also being obedient to God because we are loving the person, and, therefore, avoiding sin. It is possible then, to connect the thoughts and conclude that unselfish behavior leads to loving someone and loving someone is obedience to God and obedience to God is holy. Conversely, if we are impatient with someone that impatience is rooted in selfishness as we think more of ourselves than the person we are being impatient with, and we are not loving that person. If we are not loving the person we are disobeying God. If we are disobeying God we are sinning.

To summarize, the above connected thoughts are diagrammed below:

Unselfishness ⇒ Love Someone ⇒ Obedience to God ⇒ Holiness

Selfishness ⇒ Not Loving Someone ⇒ Disobedience to God ⇒ Sin

We can accurately conclude that what prevents us from loving someone is selfishness. For example, if you become aware that a person has lied to you, or has lied to someone else about you, there can be two reactions. One is loving and one is not. The unloving reaction is to become offended because the lie is perceived as "the person who lied to me or about me did something unfair to me." The offended feeling may grow into bitterness or hatred toward the person who lied. If bitterness or hatred enters your thinking about the person who lied, it will not only prevent you from loving the person, but you will be sinning. The important wisdom to be learned here is that our sin can be a direct result of a perceived injustice we experienced because of another person's sin. In this example, the unfairness is that someone whom we trusted lied to us or told someone else an untruth about us. As human beings with emotions, it is perfectly natural to feel hurt if someone lies to us or about us. However, how we manage our thoughts about the hurt is the point at which we will go down a sinful (unloving) path or holy (loving) path.

The loving reaction to the hurt would be to ask God to help you love the person who lied to you or about you and to forgive them. A loving reaction is to have nothing but compassion for the person who lied. In other words, we would only focus on acknowledging that what the person did is sin and that sin will harm him/herself by separating themselves from God. If the sinful behavior becomes a life habit, the separation from God will likely be eternal. We should not want temporary or permanent separation from God for any person, hence the compassion. Furthermore, to love the person who lied, our thoughts must be more influenced and controlled by compassion and concern for them and less influenced by dwelling upon our hurt. We cannot do this on our own as we possess a sin nature. In the book of 1 Peter, chapter 2, verse 19, God tells us that, "it is commendable if a man bears up under the pain of unjust suffering because he is conscious of God." Within this verse is the key to how we can have compassion instead of bitterness or hate toward the person who lied to or about us. We can withstand the pain of unjust suffering, and have the freedom to love the person who hurt us by uniting ourselves with God. Uniting ourselves with God gives us access to His love. When we are united with God, His love becomes an overwhelming force in our lives, giving every one of our thoughts a holy cleansing by the power that accompanies His love. When this happens, our minds are filled with love, we are motivated by love, we find it easy to love, and we experience the fullness of joy because of the work of God's love in and through us.

You may be asking yourself, if I believe what has been shared in this chapter so far, how is it carried out each day in my life? In other words, what is the practical application on a daily basis? When our minds are filled with loving thoughts, we experience joy, as long as these loving thoughts are a direct result of Agape love in us. For clarification, let's assume there is a particular vehicle make and model that you would love to own and drive. Let's further assume that you purchase the vehicle. As soon as you get into the vehicle for the first time as the owner, you will experience happiness. Some people call this joy, but it is clearly not joy. When circumstances are positive in our life, we become happy. When circumstances are negative in our life, we are likely not very happy. In the former case, we have an extra bounce in our step or increased energy. In the latter case, we become stressed, or if the negative circumstances in our life linger for a long period of time, we could become depressed. Our temporary happiness or unhappiness is controlled by circumstances, but joy is possible only by the power and experience of God's love moving in and through us. Two of my children were born on Christmas Eve, but many years apart. One of them, my daughter, decided that for her 8th birthday she wanted to feed the homeless. There is no way we would not honor her request, so Melissa and I made arrangements and our family helped feed the homeless on Christmas Eve morning. The joy we experienced that day was not comparable to temporary happiness derived from positive circumstances. This joy was the direct result of loving others with God's love. Each person in our family who served will never forget the joy we experienced that Christmas Eve morning when we helped feed the homeless. Furthermore, once you have experienced joy from God's love working in and through you, you want it all the time. That desire will motivate you to continue to love others the way God loves us.

How much does God love us? He loves us to the point of dying for us. And, as discussed earlier, God tells us that laying down your life for another is the greatest love. So, one test to determine whether or not we are loving with God's love (which is the greatest love) is to ask ourselves if we are willing to die for another person. Forgiving someone is sometimes difficult, dying for them is another matter. Jesus has done both for us.

Earlier we mentioned that uniting ourselves with God enables us to love others with Agape love. How do we unite ourselves with God? Unity with God is achieved by knowing Him as God and Savior, obeying His commandments, loving Him wholeheartedly, and loving others as ourselves. God loves all people. He created all people and loves His creation (refer to the book of Genesis chapters 1 and 2). To be in spiritual unity with someone, you must not be them but be aligned with them in several ways. You must share a common understanding of basic truths. You must adhere to similar moral values. You must love the person completely. The love we are talking about is Agape love and comes only from God. Since God is Agape love, it is His nature to love others. There is a fourth component of spiritual unity that is the most difficult to understand but explains the depth of this unity and the only way it is possible. In the spiritual dimension, our soul is united with another when God's Holy Spirit enables that to happen. This unitedness is because of the criteria discussed above (common knowledge of basic truths, moral values, and loving completely). This unitedness is not oneness as with a marriage, but a bond that begins with unity of thought. This is best conveyed to us in the book of Philippians, chapter 2, verses 1-4. God says, "If you have any encouragement from being united with Christ, if any comfort from His love, if any fellowship with the Spirit, if any tenderness and compassion then make my joy complete by being like-minded, having the same love, being one in spirit and purpose. Do nothing out of selfish ambition or vain conceit, but in humility consider others better than yourselves. Each of you should look not only to your own interests, but also to the interests of others." There is a lot to consider in this passage of scripture. Please notice that oneness with another cannot be accomplished without the Holy Spirit's intervention enabling us to love completely (Agape love). Evidence of this Agape love is unselfishness toward the person we love, considering their interests instead of our own. The other components of unity are the like-minded characteristics of common knowledge of basic truths and moral values. These latter components can be shared by any two people, regardless of whether they believe in God or not. However, apart from God's (Agape) love, this can be called secular unity. People can still enjoy unity of thought, but without being able share Agape love, a person will never fully love the person they have secular unity with and, therefore, also miss experiencing joy. Remember, happiness is based upon circumstances and your perspective regarding those circumstances, joy is much deeper and comes only from loving as God loves.

The above spiritual unity with others differs from complete spiritual oneness, which is reserved for marriage and our relationship with God. God gives a wonderful illustration of this unity with Him in the book of John, chapter 3, verse 29. He compares us to a bride while He is the bridegroom. There is no deeper union between two people than a marriage. Furthermore, becoming one with another is only achievable through marriage, orchestrated in the spiritual realm. In a similar manner, we become united with God as we acknowledge Him for who He is and praise Him for what He has done for us. In essence, we are loving Him fervently. We never take on His attributes as our own, for to say or believe that would be heresy and blasphemy. For us to be unified with God, we must love as He does. Since it is not our nature to love as He does because we were born with a sin nature, we can only accomplish this by allowing Him to work through us. When He works through us, spiritual unity (oneness) with Him exists. Again, we do not in any manner become Him, but He in us enables us to love as He does.

So how is it that we can experience God's love working through us but not take on His nature? We were born as imperfect people with a nature that is inherently selfish and sinful. By humbly asking Him to not only be our savior but acknowledge that we need His nature/His love working in us to overcome the propensity toward evil that human beings possess, we are opening the door of our heart (soul). God's nature simply overcomes our nature when we ask for His will to be done in our lives. His Holy Spirit fills us and resides with our spirit to empower us with His love. His will can only be carried out in our lives if we begin to renew our minds. The book of Romans, chapter 12 discusses the need to renew our minds. This renewal is a literal transformation in thinking and getting a firm grasp on Biblical/Spiritual truths, one of which is training ourselves to be a conduit of God's love. Being a conduit of God's love is not difficult, but takes discipline and a strong desire to love. The starting point to being a conduit of God's love is realizing how much God loves us and commands us to love. He knows that our lives will be enhanced in a dynamic manner (more holiness and less sin) if we learn to love others with His love. We should remind ourselves that we must be obedient to His commands, the greatest of these is to love God with all our heart, mind, and soul and love our neighbors as ourselves. Obedience to His commands takes discipline and a mind that is convinced of the rewards of associated with obedience to God's commands. Ultimately, we must be motivated by our love for God and the prospect of becoming united with Him.

CHAPTER 4

God-Centered vs. Self-Centered

Each human being has literally millions of decisions to make during their lifetime. These decisions are more difficult as the number of choices and factors that pertain to the decision increases. For example, a decision that we make every day is what clothes to wear. As we make that decision we typically consider the following factors. What is planned for today (am I going to work, to school, to church, to watch a sporting event or movie, to paint a room in my home, etc.) or are there no plans at all? If I will be leaving my home, the weather is a relevant factor. Most of us dress differently in the summer than in the winter, unless we happen to live in a geographical location that possesses a very consistent climate like Hawaii. For some of us, what was worn yesterday may be a factor that influences our clothing decision today. Color preference is a factor in what we choose to wear. Coordinating shoes and other accessories are additional considerations in putting together our daily attire. I am confident you could name several other factors. On top of all these factors, there are certain choices. For example, if you are going to the movies and you want to wear blue jeans, and you only have one clean pair of blue jeans, the decision is easy. If you have ten pair of clean blue jeans, the decision is a bit more involved. You then have additional factors to contemplate such as which blue jeans fit the best or which am I most comfortable wearing. A discussion regarding the decision of what clothing to wear could likely consume an entire chapter in and of itself!

A good example of the number of choices affecting our decision is the grocery store. Just walk down almost any aisle in the grocery store and look at the choices of food items. Depending on your mindset, choosing a food item may be very simple or somewhat complicated. Many people have no restrictions on what they eat, and are only motivated by past eating habits and what their taste buds are accustomed to enjoy. A person's income level may also have been a factor in forming past eating habits. For these folks, a food item choice is simplified. However, some folks have other factors to consider. If you have a health concern and your doctor restricts your diet to avoid certain items that would be unhealthful to you, you will have to be more careful in choosing food items. If your budget is robust, you have more food choices. If you have had the experience of taking one or more younger children with you to the grocery store, you can easily observe what so many choices can do to a person's thinking process. I recently walked down the cereal aisle with my three youngest children. If I allowed them to choose any cereal on the shelf, one of them would have chosen in about the time it took to find the specific item they had in mind. The second child would have asked me my opinion to help guide the decision. And, if I allowed the third child to choose without any restrictions, we may still be in the grocery store. So, from this example, you can see how personality, desire, and information affects our decision-making thinking.

The above examples are obviously not major life decisions. Examples of major life decisions include, "Whom shall I marry?", or "Which home should I buy?", or "Which career should I pursue?" Most people would agree that major decisions are certainly more important than minor decisions inasmuch as what we choose when making a major decision will have a more significant effect on our life. In other words, the benefits or consequences of major decisions will have longer-term ramifications in our life than the outcomes associated with minor decisions. Hence, it is logical to conclude that most people would agree we should take more time analyzing the factors that may influence a major decision before making the decision. We began this book by discussing the things that affect our belief or unbelief in God. The decision to believe or not believe in God or some intelligent designer of the universe is not only a major decision, but one that has massive and eternal ramifications. In addition to the enormous difference in where a person spends eternity (a subject to be discussed in chapter 11 of this book) that is dictated by the decision to believe and have faith in the true God or not, this decision will also construct in a person's mind a God-centered or self-centered perspective. It is vital to understand how focusing on God vs. focusing on ourselves will impact everything we do. Much of the previous chapter had been devoted to explaining how we can love others completely only with a God-centered perspective and connection with God. The rest of this chapter will contain examples of a person's reaction to hypothetical life circumstances based upon their God-centered or self-centered perspective. The reaction to the circumstances is always accompanied by a decision or decisions that a person makes, which, in turn, will result in specific behavior.

A family member (we will assume this family member is a cousin and give this cousin the name "Red" in this example) spends a couple of weeks at your home during the summer. Let's further assume you do not know Red well as he has been a distant cousin your entire life to this point in time. During the stay, Red never volunteers to help in any way. Furthermore, Red expects three meals per day to be provided by the host (you). Red expects you to wash his clothes and take him to visit entertainment sites in the vicinity of your home. As the two weeks progress, you never hear even a hint of gratefulness from Red, nor sentiment that he will return the favor someday. It is clear that Red is taking advantage of your hospitality and generosity merely based upon the fact that you and Red have a family tie. As the two weeks come to an end, Red mentions to you that he is short of funds and requires airfare from you so that he can return to his home. There is no indication that he intends to repay you but merely implies that without airfare he is essentially stranded at your home. Now that you have the facts of this hypothetical example, let's discuss your reaction to the circumstances.

Whether you have a God-centered or self-centered perspective you have demonstrated hospitality. Whether you have a God-centered or self-centered perspective all people possess an innate knowledge of fairness and know when we experience unfairness. In the case of our houseguest Red, whether you have a God-centered or self-centered perspective, it is easy to feel you have been treated unfairly and been taken advantage of by your hypothetical cousin. Feelings associated with unfairness toward ourselves by others include dismay due to the fact that we would not expect the behavior demonstrated by Red and disbelief that someone would come to our home and treat us as Red treated us. When we perceive unfairness toward ourselves, we can become offended. This feeling of being offended can lead to some very destructive and negative thoughts and behavior. We can become annoyed with the person who offended us. We can become resentful of the person who offended us. These feelings can develop into bitterness toward the person who offended us. We can also become angry with the person who offended us. It is easy to see that the genesis of the negative feelings is directly linked to the perceived unfairness and simultaneous thoughts of offense within ourselves. That brings us to our reaction to the thoughts within ourselves. If we have a self-centered perspective, the negative feelings associated with being offended will lead to reactions that are not holy. These reactions may include thoughts like, "I cannot wait until Red leaves my home and I will never see him again", or "Red is the biggest loser I have ever met", or "The audacity of Red to expect what he expects from me is not only bold and rude, but lacking respect for me." These thoughts may turn into actions such as angrily kicking Red out of your home or gossiping about Red to other family members or friends. None of the foregoing thoughts or reactions are holy nor how God would want us to think or act. For the person who has a God-centered perspective and, therefore, filled with God's Holy Spirit which enables us to love even our enemies (as discussed in chapter 3), the reaction to Red can be very different than the self-centered perspective. If we have Agape love flowing through us, we will take the thoughts generated by the unfairness done to us by Red and run them through a lens of love. What does this mean? We will react with compassion toward Red. We will try to understand why he is treating us the way he is during his stay at our home. We may find that he was raised without instruction regarding respecting others and serving others. We realize that Red was born, as we all were, with a sin nature, and he may not have had the example of God-centered parents to provide an impartation of wisdom and love. Or, he may have never thought much of the existence of God and how his life could be filled with joy if he would connect with God, thereby enabling him to love others. Whatever influences Red to act the way he does, we can help him. Being God-centered, we should first pray for Red and ask God to intervene in this situation. Filled with Agape love for Red, we would sit down with him and have a heart to heart talk about the expectations he has during his visit and reach a mutual understanding of expectations that the two of us can live with to optimize the visit in a positive manner. For example, we could discuss that when we share meals at the home, preparing the meals and cleaning up after we are finished eating is to be a joint effort. Some of the discussion with Red could be uncomfortable for one or both parties, however, if approached in love by the person feeling offended, positive outcomes are essentially guaranteed. How can I be so sure of that? Because, it is a promise from God. In the book of Proverbs, chapter 16, verse 7, God tells us that, "When a man's ways are pleasing to the Lord, he makes even his enemies live at peace with him." Due solely to the power of Agape love, we can act in a manner pleasing to God. When we do please God with our actions, those actions directed toward others will be filled with the byproduct of peace. As if peace among people we interact with was not positive enough, there are three other powerful benefits of loving others. One is experiencing joy. How that occurs was discussed in the preceding chapter. How we are sure that occurs can be emphasized by much scripture. The book of Proverbs, chapter 12, verse 20 states, "There is deceit in the hearts of those who plot evil, but joy for those who promote peace." As we promote peace with others, we are loving them. As we love others, we experience joy. When we experience that joy it is an enormous strength to us. The second benefit of loving others is righteousness. In the book of James, chapter 3, verse 18, God tells us, "Peacemakers who sow in peace raise a harvest of righteousness." As we love others, we are being peacemakers. The peace that we give is like seed planted by us into the person to whom we are giving peace. The seed are seeds of love. We gain righteousness for ourselves because we are acting in a morally pure manner. The third benefit of loving others is that as we love, we are being sanctified by God. The book of 1 Thessalonians, chapter 5, verse 23, tells us, "May God Himself, the God of peace, sanctify you through and through. May your whole spirit, soul, and body be kept blameless at the coming of our Lord Jesus." As we love others with His Agape love, God is sanctifying us, which is the process of conditioning us to live a holy life. He does this for our benefit and as a way of spreading the truth of who He is to all people. He knows we cannot love others with Agape love or be sanctified without Him, which is why He gave us His Holy Spirit to dwell within ourselves alongside our spirit and soul.

Let's turn our attention to a second example of hypothetical circumstances and the inappropriate and appropriate reactions to those circumstances. The second example is something we have discussed and the sin that could occur as a result of our reaction. This time I want to take the thought a bit further. This example is something that almost all adults who drive experience, particularly if the driver lives or drives in a city prone to moderate to heavy traffic conditions. Let's assume you are driving in heavy traffic and are running a bit late for work because the traffic is heavier than usual. Let's further assume that other drivers are aggressively driving on the shoulder of the road and looking to bypass as many cars as possible and then enter the driving lane. One of these drivers, whom we will call Rudy, is attempting to enter the driving lane and wants to "cut in" right in front of your car. There are several reactions to this situation that may occur. First, let's talk about a reaction of someone who is self-centered.

Much like the previous example of our temporary house guest Red, feelings of unfairness and even rudeness may be initial thoughts to the actions of the driver attempting to bypass a long line of traffic. In this case, the phrase "why does this person think they have the right to pass me?" may sum up the most common thought. If we are focused upon ourselves, those feelings can lead directly to anger and immediate retaliation. The retaliation may be speeding up to prevent the perceived "driving cheater" Rudy into the long line of vehicles who are abiding by the rules. In more extreme reactions, we may let the offensive driver know how we feel by a long horn honk, swerving, or tailgating and/or flashing your headlights if Rudy does happen to "cut in" directly in front of you. Of course, the danger in any of these forms of retaliation is that the tension between you and Rudy escalates, which could result in a very bad situation for both parties involved.

If we are God-centered and focused on loving others, we will take the initial feelings of the unfairness and rudeness about what the driver Rudy is attempting to do and, by the power of God's love, stop those thoughts in their tracks before those feelings grow into sinful thoughts, and potentially, sinful behavior. The key phrase in the preceding sentence is "by the power of God's love"; the same love that enables us to have compassion for our house guest Red in the first example and that provides us with the capability of loving even our enemies. So, what behavior can we demonstrate that will show Rudy we are thinking more of him than ourselves? We could immediately slow our vehicle or stop to let him in the driving lane. We could also wave to him accompanied by a kind smile, rather than sarcasm or disgust written all over our faces. The latter could possibly be the case if we were focused on ourselves. Ultimately, we do not know if our behavior motivated by love will change the future behavior of Rudy for the better, however, what we do accomplish is avoiding an escalation of negative thoughts and feelings and potential destructive actions by both parties. Showing love to others, particularly at times when it is not expected, will send a subtle message that reverberates within the recipient's soul. The message can range from astonishment, if the recipient of love has done a significant injustice to the person giving the love, to at least making the person who perceives they did nothing to deserve the love to dwell, even if briefly, upon why the love was generously and freely given.

The third example involves inappropriate communication using social media. Most people agree that as our society has increasingly utilized social media to communicate, society, in general, is much more likely to abandon civility and respect in those communications. In other words, people perceive they have more freedom to send messages of hate, belittlement, discouragement, sarcasm, and cynicism than they would if they were communicating with the same individual face to face or even through a live phone call. The sender of hate messages can hide behind their electronic device, particularly when they have never even met the person they are sending a message to. Furthermore, hate messages can happen among people who have met, even if the sender and recipient of the hate message are considered friends or relatives. These messages containing hate are so prevalent that an Internet slang word has been created to describe the event. The word is trolling and the troll is a person who intentionally stirs up emotions, many times to directly hurt someone's feelings or start an argument or illicit a negative response of some kind. This behavior by the "troll" is considered online harassment. In fact, "trolling" can be used to sabotage someone. For example, a "troll" may make up stories about a person to tarnish their reputation and prevent them from a certain achievement. We will assume that you are well liked at your place of employment because of your work ethic (you give maximum effort each day and, in fact, usually go above and beyond what is expected), your positive outlook (an attitude of believing that there is no challenge too large and no obstacle that is insurmountable), and your willingness to help co-workers (even if it means taking time away from your own productivity). You are viewed favorably by managers and have received two promotions over the past three years. The second promotion was accompanied by a generous gift given to you by your employer. You and your family were given a week on Maui, one of the Hawaiian islands. All expenses were paid by your employer. There is one particular co-worker who becomes jealous of your success. Their jealous feelings turn to bitterness and anger toward you. We will name the jealous employee Capo. The bitterness and jealousy get the best of Capo. His behavior at your place of employment has become increasing unpredictable and outrageous recently. Capo begins to send anonymous letters to various senior members of the company with disturbing accusations about you. He orchestrates a fierce attack against you on social media via trolling and recruiting a few accomplices to support the lies about you that he posts on the Internet. These accusations are investigated by the company's Human Resources department and all accusations made by Capo are unsubstantiated. Capo sees that his efforts to tarnish your reputation are in vain, which only increases the anger within Capo toward you. Capo's inability to advance his own career due to sub-standard performance leaves him with an income that is often insufficient to meet the basic needs of his family and contributes to the level of anger toward you. One day, Capo's out of control anger toward you manifests itself in Capo threatening to harm you. You report Capo's behavior to the Human Resources department. After meeting with you and Capo separately, both of you meet with Vice President of Human Resources together. In an attempt to diffuse the animosity displayed by Capo toward you, the Vice President of Human Resources believes it is important for Capo to hear directly from you. So, the Vice President of Human Resources invites you to let Capo know how you feel. What do you say to him? Let's examine the thinking behind what you might say to Capo based upon your self-centered or God-centered perspective.

If you had a self-centered perspective, you would be inclined to let your anger control your actions. With that perspective in mind, if someone threatens you with actual or implied physical harm, you would have thoughts such as, "What did I do to deserve this?" and "I need to teach this person a lesson". The latter being the retaliatory type thinking we discussed in an earlier example. You may make statements to Capo that do not soothe feelings but exacerbates the tension. For example, you may defend your innocence by issuing a verbal attack saying, "Who do you think you are to threaten me when I have done nothing to offend you in any way?" or "Your behavior tells me that you need psychological help!" or "All I want is for you to leave me alone so let's act like neither of us knows the other person exists." These types of responses to Capo will only serve to further divide the two of you because there is a complete absence of love in each statement.

If you are God-centered and have become accustomed to loving others (even those who treat you unfairly or display hate toward you), your message to Capo will reflect Agape love. As in previous examples, you will have compassion for Capo. An appropriate response to Capo would be, "I'm truly sorry you believe that the way I have lived my professional life has affected your life negatively." "I always want the best for others, including you." "When people take the time to work together, good things happen." "I would enjoy getting together once a week at lunch to talk about how I approach areas of my job and those discussions may help you as you seek to advance your career." What is the common communication message to each person who offended us in these first three examples? The answer is that we showed Red, Rudy, and Capo that we care more about them than the circumstances that took place between us. Furthermore, the reason we are able to show concern and compassion for them in spite of the circumstances is that we are not focused on self, but on God, who enables us to love abundantly and deeper to the point of rendering the circumstances ineffective in terms of producing a negative reaction from us.

The fourth example of hypothetical circumstances involves children's sporting events. One joy in my life has been to play and coach sports. More specifically, coach Little League baseball. The younger the children, the more fun it has been. Almost anyone knows a child who has participated in youth sports or has attended a youth sports event will easily relate to the following circumstances. The spring coach pitch baseball season is winding down and the weather is warming up as summer approaches. The air temperature is not the only thing warming up. The 7 and 8 year old boys are enjoying hitting the thrown baseball vs. hitting off the batting tee in past seasons. This particular evening, the Yankees are playing the Red Sox. Both teams are having a lot of fun in a very close game. One of the Red Sox players hits a ball all the way past the outfielders head and the ball rolls to the fence at the far edge of the outfield. The Yankee outfielder runs to the ball and throws the ball toward the infield. The Yankee shortstop catches the ball and throws the ball to the Yankee who is playing the catcher position standing at home base. The Yankee standing at home base catches the ball just in time to tag the Red Sox runner out as he runs toward home base (the Red Sox runner does not attempt to slide into home base). When tagged by the Yankee catcher, the Red Sox runner falls down and is called out by the umpire. The Red Sox runner has both his feelings and his backside bruised as a result of this play at home base. He begins to cry as he walks slowly back to the Red Sox dugout. The father of the Red Sox runner shouts loudly at the umpire that his son should be called safe inasmuch as the catcher intentionally tried to hurt the runner. The umpire ignores the father's protest, but the father does not stop. In addition, the Red Sox coach runs out to the umpire to issue a similar complaint about the collision at home base between the two players. The umpire calmly tells the coach that his decision on the play has been made and for the coach to return to the dugout so the game can continue. By this time the father of the boy makes his way onto the field and continues to verbally harass the umpire. The Yankee coach is watching all of this and gathers his team. What should the coach of the Yankees do?

With a self-centered perspective, the reaction of the Yankee coach would be to let the three men continue their argument, maybe hoping that the coach of the Red Sox and the father will be thrown out of the game and told to leave the baseball field. That thoughts of, "I hope the coach of the Red Sox and the father of the runner get what they deserve", or "If the coach is thrown out of the game, the chances of the Yankees winning the game improves." On top of these thoughts, the coach of the Yankees sits idly by doing nothing to help resolve the situation.

If the coach of the Yankees had a God-centered perspective, he would ask God for patience and wisdom and walk to the place where the three men are arguing. Once he gets there, he should communicate to all parties that we can resolve this situation very easily. He should calmly ask that he be given an opportunity to make a suggestion in the interest of achieving the best possible outcome for everyone. The Yankee coach could then say, "I understand how all of you feel." To the runner's father he would say, "As a father, I know you want to ensure your son is treated fairly and not endangered intentionally." To the Red Sox coach, he would say, "I understand why you are upset and I want to show you that, as a good faith gesture, we can resolve this issue."

To the umpire, he would say, "You do not deserve to be yelled at, I understand you are just doing your job and made the call that the rules dictate." To all three of them, he would say, "Listen, gentlemen, this is not worth getting upset about. I propose the Red Sox runner be given another chance to hit, essentially, nullifying what just happened." The Yankees had no obligation to allow the Red Sox batter to go to bat again and not count the out that was just made. However, when we bend the line of fairness between two people in favor of another person, we are extending Agape love to that person. We are communicating to that person that he/she is more important than the circumstances, in this case, a baseball game. The person who receives fairness beyond what is required under the circumstances is touched by Agape love.

You can see from these examples a clear distinction in words and actions between a person with a self-centered perspective and a person with a God-centered perspective. The delivery of Agape love to others is powerful in terms of neutralizing heightened negative emotions that previously existed in the mind of the recipient of the Agape love. In addition, the delivery of Agape love stifles potentially harmful or explosive action, before it occurs. Thirdly, the delivery of Agape love makes the recipient realize that someone cares about them, and maybe, just maybe, that thought will blossom into a changed perspective for the person receiving the love. When that does happen, the result is accomplishing the will of God. For the person delivering Agape love, there is immense joy experienced per our discussion earlier in this book. There is nothing that compares to that joy because it is generated by God's love at work through you. In the book of Romans, chapter 5, verses 1-5, the God tells us, "Therefore, we have been justified through faith, we have peace with God through our Lord, Jesus Christ, though whom we have gained access by faith into this grace in which we now stand. And, we rejoice in the hope of the glory of God. Not only so, but we also rejoice in our sufferings, because we know that suffering produces perseverance; perseverance, character; and character, hope. And hope does not disappoint us, because God has poured out His love into our hearts by the Holy Spirit, whom He has given us." There is much to be gleaned from this passage of scripture. God refers to us being "justified by faith". We can only be justified by faith if we have faith in God. Not just faith in a god, but faith in the one true God and the fact that Jesus Christ came to earth and died for us to atone for our sin. Why do we have to be justified? Each person has the choice to believe or not believe. If we believe in what Jesus Christ did and that He is God, that faith is the justification for God removing the penalty we would have earned and received because of our sin. The penalty for sin is eternal death; removal of that penalty means we are rewarded with eternal life. The passage also mentions that peace with God accompanies this justification. Sin separates us from God. When we sin, we are disobeying God. When we disobey God, there cannot be peace between ourselves and God. If a child disobeys his or her parent, the child has guilt and the parent is at the very least disappointed that the child disobeyed. Both child and parent are experiencing a lack of peace between them. Peace is restored between parent and child when the parent forgives the child and the child is truly sorry for their disobedience. So it is with ourselves and God. The scripture also refers to "grace in which we now stand."

That grace is God's forgiveness of our sin given freely and in spite of the fact that it is undeserved. We obtain His grace, or favor, through faith. The next sentence in the passage reads, "And, we rejoice in the hope of the glory of God." The hope possessed by those who believe is rooted in their faith. A believer knows that God not only exists, but, because He loves us so much, has forgiven us. Our hope is not characterized as thinking about the future with any amount of uncertainty, but rather an unshakeable expectation that the future will hold all that we believe. Hope is the expectation of what will happen in the future and faith is the assurance of that hope. Convinced of a future that includes eternal life in a perfect place is the reason we rejoice! Who wouldn't? Well, believe it or not many who believe in God and eternal life do not rejoice inasmuch as their perspective is focused on life on earth in the present moment rather than what is to come. If, one spring you plan a family summer vacation to a destination that you never thought possible, but is now a reality, each member of the family will look forward to the vacation with excitement. Each family member will live each day between now and when the vacation begins doing what needs to be done (for example, going to work or school), but in the mind of each family member they cannot help but think about the vacation a few months away. And, each time they do, feelings of happiness invade their minds. It is the anticipation and expectation of an extremely positive future event that brings us to the point of rejoicing. In the case of eternal life, there is not a greater future event......so, we rejoice! The passage goes on to say that, "we also rejoice in our sufferings, because we know that suffering produces perseverance; perseverance, character; and character, hope". For many, the concept of rejoicing in our suffering seems very odd and certainly unrealistic and unachievable. After all, no one wants to suffer, so how can we rejoice when it happens? We can rejoice by realizing that even during times of suffering for our beliefs (largely due to attacks from those who hate Jesus), our steadfast faith will enable us to persevere, and when we persevere, our character is strengthened, and when our character is strengthened, so is our hope. When circumstances occur in our lives that confirm what we had previously hoped for is going to occur, we rejoice. That is the case with suffering. We have been told by God that the world will hate us because of Him. In the example of the family vacation that we are excited about, if the airline tickets are purchased and we see an email confirmation of the tickets, the realization of the trip becomes more tangible and we get even more excited with anticipation of what is to come. The final portion of the scripture passage in Romans, chapter 5 quoted above states, "And hope does not disappoint us, because God has poured out His love into our hearts by the Holy Spirit, whom He has given us." As what we hope for comes to pass, both on earth and in heaven, we are vindicated (our hope did not disappoint us) from the falsehoods that those who hate us say about us or about what we believe, and we acknowledge the validation of what we believe through how we live our lives. The latter part of the previous sentence means we continue to live our lives in a God-centered manner, empowered by God's love that works through us by the Holy Spirit. Think about how privileged we are to serve a God that desires to work through us and how the mildest touch of the living God flowing through us creates a joy like nothing else we can experience. That joy strengthens us so that we are able to withstand any troubles that we encounter during our life on earth. What a demonstration of God's love for us in that He wants to work through us so that we may experience the fullness of His joy.

Now that we understand what God-centered and self-centered perspectives are and the impact that each perspective can have on how we handle various situations we encounter in life, in the next chapter we will discuss the other benefits of the power of God's love working through us.

CHAPTER 5

Self-Control and Self-Discipline

Self-control is defined as the ability to control one's emotions and desires, or the expression of them, in one's behavior. Self-discipline is defined as the ability to control one's feelings and overcome one's weaknesses; the ability to pursue what one believes is right despite temptations to abandon it. Both of these terms imply, when present in our lives, that we are able to restrain ourselves from doing something that would be harmful to ourselves or others in some way. We substitute positive, loving, holy behavior for the negative, unloving, and sinful behavior that we were tempted to act upon. In essence, we defeat temptation through self-control and self-discipline.

The most obvious example of a product of self-control is patience. Self-control is evident when we are patient in spite of our emotions pushing us not to be patient. Every person can attest to the fact that self-control regarding patience takes a certain internal fortitude, or strength, that allows us to capture the heightened emotions and render them ineffective in terms of creating negative thoughts and actions.

To better understand this subject of capturing heightened emotions, we will explore a bit more about how thoughts and emotions and feelings are related. And, of course, we will do so by analyzing the truths that God, who knows us best, has revealed to us.

First, think about what God says about the subject of controlling emotions. In chapter 2 of this book, we cited a passage of scripture in the second book of Corinthians regarding taking every thought captive. If you take every thought captive, you have put a holy filter on each thought. Doing so will lead to positive emotional reactions and subdued negative emotional reactions. Positive emotional reactions result in positive feelings tied to those emotions. The converse, of course, is true of negative emotional reactions and negative feelings. Lastly, the positive feelings will lead to positive actions. The negative feelings typically lead to negative actions. With God, we have the power to stop the process from progressing down a negative path and stay within the positive path. We covered spiritual forces earlier in this book. Since that discussion in chapter 2 about spiritual forces, we have covered the power of God's love and keeping our perspective on God instead of on ourselves. If you think about any day in your life from the moment you wake up to the moment you go to sleep you will find hundreds of times that your thoughts will affect your emotions. Your mind is bombarded with thousands of external stimuli that are processed. When these stimuli are processed, the product of the processing is the formation of a thought. The thought that is generated will then give rise to a certain emotion. There are many types of emotions and intensities of those emotions. The rise of the emotion will create a state of mind within us. That state of mind will affect our behavior. So, how do feelings fit into this discussion? A feeling is an emotional state of mind. As an example, if your wife called you to tell you she is pregnant and you have wanted to have a child for a long time, you would hang up the phone and everyone around you would know you are feeling ecstatic. You listened to your wife as she told you the fact that she became pregnant. As you listened, her words were processed and became thoughts in your mind. As you reflected upon those thoughts and realized what they meant, your emotional level rose dramatically, resulting in an intense feeling of happiness. Would that feeling have led to an action? You bet. You may have picked up flowers on the way home or made a reservation for the two of you to go out to dinner and celebrate.

Let's summarize the relationship between thoughts, emotions, feelings, and actions through the following steps.

Step 1: We become aware of stimuli in our life through one of our senses (see, hear, touch, taste, or smell).

Step 2: The stimuli are processed and **thoughts** are created.

Step 3: The **thoughts** created will impact our **emotions**.

Step 4: Our **emotions** will result in **feelings** that will impact our **actions**.

Sometimes, the effect of the stimuli will be positive and sometimes the effect of the stimuli will be negative. There may also be stimuli that have a neutral effect, but thoughts that have a neutral effect will not impact our behavior so it is not important to spend time managing our thoughts and responses related to a neutral thought.

An important factor that drives how we process stimuli to create a thought and the intensity of the associated reaction is our prior experience with, or feelings toward, an element of the stimuli. For example, if you love ice cream and just learned that tomorrow is national ice cream day and that your favorite ice cream store is selling all items for 50% off, you will have a positive thought, your emotional reaction will result in a feeling of happiness, and you will likely plan to stop by the ice cream store to take them up on the deal they are offering. If, however, you do not like ice cream, you will likely have a neutral thought regarding the ice cream sale in as much as the thought of eating ice cream is not appealing to you. If you love ice cream but you cannot eat it due to some health issue, you will likely have a negative thought about the news of the ice cream sale inasmuch as you are unable to partake in something you love.

The same principle works if the stimuli are people. Let's assume something very positive (the birth of a healthy child) is experienced by a set of parents. If the happy event happens to your good friend or a close family member with whom you have a wonderful relationship, your thoughts will be positive and you will wholeheartedly share in the happiness your good friend or close family member is experiencing. If the same event happens to a person who has hurt you repeatedly, your negative thoughts about the person will prevent you from not only sharing in their happiness, but will likely cause you to have bitterness toward that person and that bitterness will interfere with your ability to love the person. Lastly, there is the neutral outcome. If you learn that someone you do not know welcomes a new child into the world, there will likely be a very subdued thought and associated reaction.

Your thoughts will often be influenced more by the stimuli than your preconceived thoughts of the person responsible for the stimuli. When this is the case, if a positive thought occurs as a result of something someone has said or done, that positive thought will influence your opinion, in a positive manner, of that person, regardless of your opinion of the person before the stimuli. In the same way, if a negative thought occurs as a result of something someone has said or done, that negative thought will influence your opinion, in a negative manner, of that person, regardless of your opinion of the person before the stimuli. For example, if someone compliments you, your immediate thought will be, "that was very nice of that person" and that thought will generate a good feeling based upon a positive emotion. Conversely, if you find out that someone gossips about you, your immediate thought will be, "why did the person say that about me?" or "that was a mean thing they did", and that thought will generate a bad feeling based upon a negative emotion. In both cases, the thoughts and feelings will influence your opinion of the person.

To further our thinking on this subject, here is another example of the effect of stimuli on our thoughts. If you collect your mail from your mailbox, open a letter received from the Internal Revenue Service (IRS) informing you that a mistake was made on your tax return and you are due a refund from the IRS of $500, the stimuli of reading the letter would lead to a positive emotion and good feeling. If, however, you collected mail from your mailbox and opened a letter from the IRS informing you that a mistake was made on your tax return and you owe the IRS $500, you would have a negative emotion and bad feeling. The links between stimuli, thought, emotion, and feeling occur systematically.

The reason it is important to understand the relationship between thoughts, emotions, feelings, and actions is that understanding helps us realize and pinpoint the point in time that we need to take the thought captive (control our reaction to the thought) as God has instructed us to do. Once we become aware of the point in time that we need to take a thought captive, we can exercise our will over the thought before the thought influences us toward a behavior that is not holy. Exercise of our will to achieve a behavioral outcome that is holy (loving) when a thought is negative, thereby tending to generate an unholy or unloving behavior, is self-control. Self-discipline if very similar. With self-discipline, we exert an intentional effort to achieve a behavior that requires us to overcome a natural force that works against us. If the natural force is not overcome it may prevent us from achieving the new, desired behavior. For example, if we decide that we want to become more physically fit, we must develop a plan. The plan will likely include eating foods that are good for our body and working out several times each week (exercising by going to the gym or running/biking outside). Assuming this behavior is different than the way we typically live each day, changing the behavior requires self-control. The process of making the desired behavior the new way we live our lives each day is self-discipline. We can only be successful in our endeavor to become more physically fit if the new behavior becomes a habit. That does not mean the new behavior transition will be easy, but when the new behavior has become a habit we wake up each day already inclined to eat healthy food and exercise. In essence, we have transformed the habits of how we used to live into the new habits of healthier living with the goal of being physically fit. These changes start with our mind and the thoughts that fill our mind.

It should be apparent that restraint is only half the equation in determining future behavior. Restraint is controlling unwanted behavior, but the unwanted behavior must be replaced with preferred or improved behavior to achieve change. When a person is convinced that the new behavior will benefit them in significant way, the recognition of those potential benefits will motivate the individual to pursue the new behavior. The ability to stick to the pursuit of new behavior is called determination. Every human being can be determined. Further, every human being can achieve change regarding any behavior. However, often we need external assistance. Fortunately, the Creator of the universe loves us so much that He is not only willing to be that assistance, but desires to be that assistance. In the book of 1 Peter, chapter 4, verse 11, God says, "If anyone serves, he should do it with the strength God provides." The book of Colossians, chapter 1, verse 11 reads "being strengthened with all power according to His glorious might so that you may have great endurance." In the book of Exodus, chapter 15, verse 2, the Word of God states, "The Lord is my strength." God wants us to know He will strengthen us if we rely on Him. That strength applies to every thought we have and every action we take. That strength helps us overcome difficult circumstances in our lives. That strength enables us to achieve positive change in our behavior.

Now, let's take what we learned about self-control and self-discipline and apply that learning to the forces at work in the spiritual realm. In chapter 2 of this book we discussed spiritual forces. These forces are constant. The forces of evil will influence us to generate negative thoughts in our minds. These negative thoughts can also be considered the genesis of sin inasmuch as these negative thoughts, if unchecked, will lead to sin. The stimuli that influence our thinking that can create these negative thoughts is temptation. These temptations are only temptations because we were born with a sin nature. In other words, without God's intervention, our natural inclination is to sin because apart from God, we typically only think of ourselves. However, the good news is that we can overcome these temptations with God's help. In fact, Jesus showed us how to overcome temptation. The book of Matthew, chapter 4 and the book of Luke, chapter 4 chronicle the time when Jesus went out to the desert and fasted for forty days. Then the king of the forces of evil, Satan, came to Jesus and tempted Him by taunting Jesus to prove He was God by turning the stones into bread. Think about how Satan tempted Jesus. He focused the temptation on an area of vulnerability given Jesus had just fasted for forty days. However, Jesus did not succumb to the temptation and told Satan, "Man does not live on bread alone, but on every word that comes from the mouth of God." Jesus was not only showing Satan that the temptation was not going to be effective, but He recited scripture to express a much deeper truth. Satan thought he would be smart and quoted scripture as part of the second attempt to tempt Jesus. Again, the temptation failed as Jesus reminded Satan to whom he was speaking when he told Satan, "It is also written, 'Do not put the Lord your God to the test.'" A third temptation came from Satan when he told Jesus that he would give Jesus all that he sees if Jesus would just bow down and worship Satan. This time Jesus ended the temptations by again quoting scripture saying, "Away from me, Satan! For it is written: 'Worship the Lord your God, and serve him only.'" This example of Jesus being tempted, and His responses to that temptation, give us valuable instruction. As Jesus did, we can avoid succumbing to temptation, not because we are as strong as He is, but because we can have access to the power to avoid temptation by submitting to Him. When we submit to Him we seek to understand more about Him. The result is we gain what we need, and what Jesus used, to defeat temptation. How did Jesus defeat temptation? By understanding His truths, using His wisdom, and showing the enemy He can resist the temptation. How do we defeat temptation? By understanding truths of God (which are revealed to us in His Word), using wisdom (which comes from God), we are enabled to show the enemy that we (with God's help) can resist the temptation. God tells us in the book of James, chapter 4, verse 7 to, "Submit yourselves, then, to God. Resist the devil, and he will flee from you." If we could see into the spiritual realm, we would see angels and demons. And, a demon who causes a particular temptation does literally leave when we resist temptation. However, the enemy hates us and will never permanently cease to bring about temptation, because he knows we are fallible and may have moments of weakness due to circumstances in our lives. Examples of circumstances that could cause weakness are the death of someone you love, a serious sickness, the loss of a job, experiencing hurt caused by another person, and divorce, just to name a few. Other factors that can make us vulnerable to temptation are fatigue, not making time for God in terms of reading His Word and praying (talking) to Him, and lack of fellowship (spending time with friends who love us and whom we love) with those who are also connected to Jesus. There are many scriptures that apply to this discussion, but a couple stand out that we want to share with you. In the book of Ephesians, chapter 6, verses 10-18, God lays out a framework for defeating temptation. Verse 10 reads, "Finally, be strong in the Lord and in his mighty power." As we discussed earlier, we need His mighty power to defeat temptation. If you are guaranteed that you will have success in something very important to you as long as you follow a few simple steps as a course of action, you would fervently pursue those steps that would lead to success. Every rational thinking person would. The same is true regarding the subject of temptation. There is nothing God's power cannot defeat. He makes that power available to us, not to possess it, but to allow His power to work in us to enable us to defeat the enemy. We just have to follow a few simple steps. Those steps are discussed in the remaining verses of the passage we cited in the book of Ephesians. Verse 11 reads, "Put on the full armor of God so that you can take your stand against the devil's schemes." The armor will be described in subsequent verses. The key truth to understand here is that if we put on the full armor of God, we will defeat temptation and anything the devil (Satan) throws at us. Putting on the armor, piece by piece, are the steps that tap into God's power and are needed to defeat temptation. In verse 12 God then goes on to explain in more depth the spiritual realm from which temptation is orchestrated. He says, "For our struggle is not against flesh and blood, but against rulers, against the authorities, against the powers of this dark world, and against the spiritual forces of evil in the heavenly realms." We have already examined spiritual forces in chapter 2 of this book, but at the risk of being a bit redundant, please understand that God is reminding us that there is a spiritual dimension filled with good and evil forces at work. A key point to be made from verse 12 is the reference to "this dark world." Throughout scripture, God refers to truth and Himself as light and evil as darkness. In this verse, God identifies our adversary as a ruler, an authority, and a power. He is reminding us that because man brought sin into the world, it became dark. We invited evil in unintentionally. We unleased a powerful force that would work against us perpetually while each of us lives on earth. And, because we typically cannot see these spiritual forces does not mean they do not exist. In the book of Hebrews, chapter 11, verse 1, God tells us that part of the definition of faith is, "being certain of what we do not see." Therefore, when He tells us about these spiritual forces that exist in a realm we do not see, we believe because our faith in God assures us that the content of His truths are real, whether or not we can physically see the spiritual dimension. Notice the terms ruler, authority, and power being used to refer to the evil forces. Since we live in this dark world, we would naturally be subservient to a ruler or authority of this dark world. And, many people are because they are obedient to evil influences. That is the natural order for those who live according to their sinful nature. God even goes as far as to say that without Him we are slaves to sin. In the book of Romans, chapter 6, verses 16-18, He says, "Don't you know that when you offer yourselves to someone to obey him as slaves, you are slaves to the one whom you obey, whether you are slaves to sin, which leads to death, or to obedience, which leads to righteousness? But thanks be to God that, though you used to be slaves to sin, you wholeheartedly obeyed the form of teaching to which you were entrusted. You have been set free from sin and have become slaves to righteousness." There are two important learnings from this passage. First, if we do obey the evil forces, we become a slave to those forces. That means we carry out sin because we are obedient to the one who tempts us. Secondly, the good news is that if we are obedient to God by doing what He says, we break free from the bondage of sin and pursue righteousness, or holiness. Obedience to God unlocks our ability to defeat sin because of

His power at work within us.

Back to Ephesians, chapter 6, picking up with verse 13 which reads, "Therefore put on the full armor of God, so that when the day of evil comes, you may be able to stand your ground, and after you have done everything, to stand." As we discuss the armor in the following verses, remember to assure ourselves of victory over temptation, we must put on the full armor, not a portion of that armor. Verses 14-18 state, "Stand firm then, with the belt of truth buckled around your waist, with the breastplate of righteousness in place, and with your feet fitted with the readiness that comes from the gospel of peace. In addition to all this, take up the shield of faith, with which you can extinguish all the flaming arrows of the evil one. Take the helmet of salvation and the sword of the Spirit, which is the word of God. And pray in the Spirit on all occasions with all kinds of prayers and requests. With this in mind, be alert and always keep on praying for all the saints." The first piece of armor (the belt of truth) refers to understanding and holding onto the truth. If you are reading this book, you are seeking to understand the truth. As you do, all God tells you is to hold on to it. Do not take truth nonchalantly, but grasp it with passion and never let it leave your mind. The second piece of armor is breastplate of righteousness. Once we know the truth, we can begin to lead a life of righteousness, or holiness. Living in a righteous or holy manner will protect us inasmuch as temptation will essentially bounce right off us because we are focused on living for and obeying God. The next piece of armor is the gospel of peace. One way we maintain strength is have peace as we go into battle. Understanding the gospel, or good news, that Jesus died for us gives us peace. The next piece of armor is the shield of faith. If we are outfitted from head to toe with armor, why would we need a shield? Because the enemy's attacks are relentless, if we take enough direct hits to our armor, we will eventually weaken. However, an unwavering faith enables us to have impenetrable protection that never fails us. The next piece of armor is the helmet of salvation. It hardly seems coincidental that salvation is represented by the helmet. We come to a state of salvation by acknowledging the truths about God in our mind. Our mind is our intellect. We, of course, have a physical brain and we possess a soul, which is the intellect of our spirit. The physical brain brings the thoughts of our soul to our consciousness. The next piece of armor is the sword of the spirit. The word of God is our sword. The sword is an offensive weapon rather than a defensive piece of equipment. The word of God is powerful and, as we saw Jesus do when temptation came, He used the word to defeat Satan. It cannot be emphasized enough that it is essential to understand God's word so that we have it readily available when temptation arrives. Reading God's word on a regular basis is sufficient, but many find that memorizing scripture makes the word an even more powerful force in our lives. Furthermore, remember that God is the word (see the book of John, chapter 1, verse 1). Lastly, God tells us, in the passage in Ephesians chapter 6, to pray in the Spirit. This concept is confusing to some and the real meaning is occasionally debated in the Christian community. The fact that the word Spirit contains a capital "S" in verse 18 means the writer is referring to the Holy Spirit, much like we have capitalized pronoun references to God in this book. The significance of a capital letter being used when we refer to God is a recognition of the Supreme Being that He is and a form of showing respect to Him. It is vital to pray, God even tells us to "pray without ceasing". Our prayers are to reflect our submission to Him and recognition of our need for Him to intervene in our lives. Praying in the Spirit goes a step further in terms of God's involvement in our prayers. He, through His Holy Spirit, will assist us in what we should be praying. This is a level of prayer that can only be obtained if we ask Him to help us pray. Many believe that praying in the Spirit means praying while speaking in tongues. There is merit in this perspective inasmuch as the Holy Spirit is not only present, but essentially takes over our prayer time and intercedes on our behalf. Please understand, though, that God is present during our prayer time, whether we are speaking our native language or a heavenly language.

When Jesus taught us to pray, He used His native language and the translation to the English language in the book of Matthew, chapter 6. Regardless of whether you use your native language or a heavenly language, the importance of prayer should not be underestimated. Prayer is a powerful weapon and a blessing to those that engage in it because, in addition to our armor and sword protecting us and helping us defeat the enemy, God responds to our need and desire for Him to act in the supernatural realm on our behalf when we ask.

Putting on the armor and praying are the primary means of defeating the temptation of sin. The reason this discussion of putting on the armor and praying is included in the chapter on self-control and self-discipline is two-fold. First, we need to control our natural tendencies to avoid holding on to the elements described in the armor and taking the time to pray. Second, it is imperative to create daily discipline in our lives that inevitably leads us to hold on to the elements described in the armor and take the time to pray. To make this happen takes effort and consistency. The process is a growth process. We will not be where we need to be initially, but with effort we will become more and more consistent. As we do, we will win more than we lose when it comes to resisting the temptation to sin.

We discussed that self-control and self-discipline involve eliminating unwanted behavior and replacing the unwanted behavior with improved behavior. The unwanted behavior occurs when we succumb to temptation. The improved behavior is holy behavior. In other words, a sinful thought or action is replaced with a holy thought or action. Every time we succeed in replacing a sinful thought with a holy thought we are being sanctified. When we experience victory over sin, the flow of God's love through us grows stronger. As we experience the flow of God's love, we are filled with joy. That joy gives us strength. The strength feeds our resolve to defeat sin again. The motivation to defeat sin drives the amount of effort we put into doing the things we need to do to constantly prepare ourselves for the next battle with sin. The battles never cease, so to consistently defeat sin we must consistently prepare ourselves. That preparation takes self-control and self-discipline.

It should now be easy to see the role self-control and self-discipline play in leading us to overcome sin. To achieve the most difficult things in life, we must be motivated by the thought that what we want to accomplish is worth the effort needed to achieve the accomplishment. Let's assume, at a young age, you take an interest in gymnastics. After a few training sessions, you dream of becoming an Olympic gymnast. So, the training sessions continue. A few months later you decide that you want to seriously pursue becoming an Olympic gymnast. There is an enormous amount of training and practice required to compete at such a high level. Knowing that, the issue that confronts you is whether or not your desire to become an Olympic gymnast is strong enough to motivate you to put in hours of work each day to accomplish your goal. So, assuming your desire is strong enough to convince yourself the effort is worth it, you begin a regimen of practice sessions each day. Your level of commitment is high because you are motivated. This phenomenon can be applied to anything we want to accomplish in life. For example, if you desire to obtain a college degree, and that desire is strong enough to persuade yourself that obtaining the degree is worth the effort needed, you will take the steps necessary to embark on the path toward pursuing a college degree. The key concept we are trying to convey is that an internal desire to want to achieve a specific outcome must be strong enough to overcome any hesitation that may exist because of a perception that the effort needed is either too great or the outcome is not possible to achieve because of a perceived lack of ability or resources. The human will is powerful. With sufficient desire, we can be motivated to strive to achieve any dream. This concept is also applicable to sin and holiness. If our desire is to overcome sin, to serve God by obeying Him, and to live a life pursuing holiness powered by God's love, we will put effort in each day to accomplish the goal. The more motivated we are, the more disciplined we will be in staying the course to accomplish our goal.

CHAPTER 6

Healthy Life Habits

As we fully comprehend the previous chapter, it is easy to see why the importance of self-control and self-discipline in our lives cannot be overstated. These traits are essential to living a life filled with healthy life habits. Developing healthy life habits means doing what is optimal for our physical bodies, our soul, and our spirit. Before describing healthy life habits in greater detail, it is important to ensure an understanding of the three entities mentioned in the preceding sentence, which are the beneficiaries of healthy life habits.

Our physical body is the easiest to understand. Upon conception, every human being has a physical body. Our body experiences extraordinary growth in utero, a Latin term meaning "in the womb." During the gestational period, the process of developing a fully functioning physical body is occurring miraculously. The science of biology has taught us much about what is happening as a physical body is being developed. Each human contains 23 pairs of chromosomes contained in cells. The main constituent of chromosomes is DNA, or deoxyribonucleic acid. This DNA contains literally billions of pieces of genetic information. This genetic information determines our physical makeup. What is most interesting to contemplate is that even though we are all unique physically, we are also 99.9% alike per the science of biology. That fact tells us how massive the process of creating life is, considering we essentially all go through the same process and an infinitesimal difference between one human being and another on a cellular level can generate large variations in what we look like, how we think, or what talents we possess. Our physical bodies have a definite beginning and a definite ending.

The other two entities we are composed of, our spirit and our soul, are often considered as one. You could think of your spirit as the real you, who dwells within the physical temporary body God gave you. Your spirit, for those who have succeeded in being obedient to God and have faith in Him, will live eternally. In other words, our spirit has a definite beginning, but no end. In the book of Luke, chapter 23, verse 46, God tells us that just before Jesus died, "Jesus called out with a loud voice, 'Father, into your hands I commit my spirit.' When He had said this, He breathed His last." In verse 43 of the same book and chapter, Jesus spoke to one of the men who was being crucified with Jesus. He told the man, "I tell you the truth, today you will be with me in paradise." We know that Jesus' physical body died, and was in a grave for a few days. We also know the physical body of the man on the cross next to Jesus died. Furthermore, we know they were together later that day. How is this possible? The spirit of Jesus and the spirit of the man on the cross next to Jesus left their respective physical bodies that day. We can accurately conclude that each of us contains a spirit. There have been some attempts to prove there is a spirit, with one of the most famous being carried out by a physician named Duncan MacDougall, from Haverhill, Massachusetts. MacDougall attempted to weigh a person's body just before and, then, at the moment of death, to determine if his hypothesis (that the body should weigh a little less at the moment of death because the spirit exits) could be proven. Dr. MacDougall believed he did prove that the body of at least one person measured a bit less at the moment of death. However, some have debated the results of the experiment. Regardless, if there is a spirit being, which God has told us there is, it really doesn't matter if the spirit weighs, in the physical dimension, anything at all.

So, how does the soul fit into this discussion? In the book of 1 Thessalonians, chapter 5, verse 23, God says, "May God Himself, the God of peace, sanctify you through and through. May your whole spirit, soul, and body be kept blameless at the coming of our Lord Jesus Christ." The fact that the spirit, soul, and body are distinct entities does not mean they are separate in every way. We know that our spirit resides in our body until the time our physical body dies. So, we can draw distinction between our physical body and our spirit being. What is our soul and how does it differ from our spirit? Our soul is the intellect of our spirit. It is what generates the thoughts and emotional thinking part of who we are. Think of it this way. In the physical body there is a brain. The brain is constantly sending signals to parts of the body to function in specific ways. In addition, the brain is a repository of every experience we have had. Just as the brain is contained in the body and the body needs the brain to function, your soul is part of your spirit being and your spirit being cannot function without your soul. Your spirit and soul cannot be separated. In the book of Deuteronomy, chapter 6, verse 5, God tell us to, "Love the Lord your God with all your heart, all your soul, and all your strength."

He says, all your **soul**, not all your **spirit**. The word used in the original Hebrew text is nephesh. Although nephesh is used 753 times in the Old Testament, and there are slightly different meanings when used in other scripture, the meaning when used in this scripture in the book of Deuteronomy is "the inner being with its thoughts and emotions." An additional and important truth is your spirit has no capacity to love without your soul. Fortunately, your spirit does have a soul, and your soul was created with emotions and the ability to have rational thought. Your soul is part of your spirit, but a distinct part. In the book of Hebrews, chapter 4, verse 12, God tells us, "For the word of God is living and active. Sharper than any double-edged sword, it penetrates even to dividing soul and spirit, joints and marrow; it judges the thoughts and attitudes of the heart." The scripture makes it clear that there is nothing deeper than dividing the soul from the spirit, just as in the physical body marrow is contained in joints (bones). When our physical bodies perish, our spirit being, with our soul intact, leaves the body. Here is an analogy that may help further our understanding of the spirit and soul. Let's say you are going to frost some recently baked Christmas cookies. You buy some white frosting and mix red food coloring into the container of white frosting. If someone walks into the room after you mix the food coloring into the white frosting and you ask them "What color frosting do you see?" They would say red frosting. Even though the white frosting and red food coloring are unique items, together they are one and cannot be separated. The same is true of your spirit and soul. Now, some scholars will debate whether your spirit contains your soul or whether your soul contains your spirit. It seems much more logical to think of your spirit being containing your spirit being's emotions and intellect than your emotions and intellect apart from your physical body containing your spirit being. However, it doesn't really matter in as much as your spirit and your soul are inseparable. Wherever one goes the other goes. And, to reiterate, they both leave your physical body simultaneously when your physical body dies. So, as we resume our discussion of healthy life habits, let's consider the full impact of these habits on our physical body and spirit being/soul. We will find that healthy life habits are virtually impossible to affect one part of who we are without affecting our whole being, or the entirety of who we are. That is a very good thing when we build healthy life habits into our daily life and a very bad thing when we ignore the need to build healthy life habits into our daily life.

When you hear the phrase 'healthy life habits', what is the first thing you think about? If you are like most people, you will think about what you put into your body. Or, that you should exercise. Or, getting the appropriate amount of sleep. Most of our thoughts when we think of healthy life habits are typically focused on our physical bodies. That is normal and can drive some people to do whatever they can to eat and drink things that are good for their bodies. Furthermore, thoughts of healthy life habits may motivate some folks to begin or resume taking part in a regular exercise routine or to get to bed an hour earlier than normal if there is a perception that the amount of sleep they typically get is not enough to promote optimal health. All of these thoughts are perfectly legitimate and should cross our minds. However, healthy life habits would not only be those things that we diligently do that are good for our physical bodies. A healthy life habit is educating ourselves to prepare for, or enhance, a career. A healthy life habit is establishing a financial budget for ourselves and sticking to it. A healthy life habit is taking care of our automobiles through regular maintenance to maximize the car's longevity and dependability and efficiency. A healthy life habit is proactively performing preventative maintenance in the home/dwelling in which you reside. All of these are life habits that are good for us. Conversely, if we fail to do these things, we are increasing the probability of something bad or very bad happening to us.

There is an enormous amount of crossover regarding healthy life habits affecting all parts of our being, not just one part. For example, if we take care of our physical bodies by eating highly nutritious food, drinking clean water and pure juice, taking vitamins and minerals to supplement our diet, exercise regularly, and get enough sleep, we will be doing the things that provide optimal functioning of our bodies. When our bodies operate in an optimal or best way, we will have more energy and become sick less often than if our bodies operate in a sub-optimal or less than the best way possible. So, how does that affect our spirit/soul? In earlier chapters of this book, we discussed spiritual forces and how to overcome the evil forces that work against us. We also discussed self-control and replacing negative behaviors with good, positive, and holy behaviors. To accomplish this, we indicated there is significant effort needed. To put forth that effort, we need energy, clarity of thought, and focus. The elements of energy, clarity of thought, and focus are enhanced when we are well rested and our bodies are functioning in the most optimal manner. Therefore, a physically healthy body will help us achieve a healthy spirit/soul. Of course, as we learned earlier in this book, we cannot do the latter without God and the power of His love. Being the conduit of God's love is vital, but that cannot happen in the most consistent manner unless we do our part! Taking care of our physical bodies is just one of the things we can do to achieve spiritual success. There is a reciprocal benefit to our physical body that comes from the positive impact on our spirit/soul as a result of having a healthy body. In the book of Proverbs, chapter 3, verses 7-8 God says, "Do not be wise in your own eyes; fear the Lord and shun evil. This will bring health to your body and nourishment to your bones." Having a healthy fear of the potential of God's wrath should drive us to shun, or turn away from, evil. In other words, turn from evil and embrace holy behaviors. In this scripture, God is telling us that if we do so, even our physical bodies will benefit. The Hebrew word etsem is used in this scripture for the term bones, which is clearly referring to our physical being. Let's take this example one step further. If we pursue holiness, as we have seen earlier in this book, we will be filled with joy. That joy is directly applicable to the following scripture. In the book of Proverbs, chapter 22, verse 17, God says, "A cheerful heart is good like medicine, but a crushed spirit dries up the bones." When we experience joy from being a conduit of God's love, the manifestation of experiencing that joy extends to our physical body. Remember, this joy is not just happiness based upon circumstances in our lives, but a deep feeling in our spirit/soul because God's love moved through us. This joyful feeling has a positive impact on our physical bodies.

To summarize the reciprocal impact of this first example, when we build healthy habits by taking care of our physical bodies, we are better equipped, by virtue of having more energy and clarity of thought, to defeat sin and pursue holy behavior. When we pursue holy behavior, we enable the flow of God's love to move in an increasingly powerful way through us, and, therefore, we receive joy. When we receive joy, a healthy environment is created or enhanced within our physical bodies and the cycle continues. This process occurs with one caveat. We must also know truth and pursue holiness. A person could be in excellent physical condition and take care of his/her physical body, but if there is no effort to pursue God, truth, and holiness, this person will not experience the manifestation of joy described above.

In the book of Leviticus, chapter 11 and in the book of Deuteronomy, chapter 14, God lists in detail what food we should eat and what food we should not eat. This instruction has nothing to do with giving a sacrificial offering to God, or denying our own desires to grow self-control within ourselves. Rather, the Creator of the universe knows what is best for our physical bodies. He also knows what is not good for our physical bodies.

He is sharing what we should and should not eat to help us maximize our physical health, which enhances our ability to experience health for our spirit/soul.

Just as healthy life habits affect the physical dimension of life (our physical bodies, the tangible things we have or use, our finances, etc.), we can develop healthy life habits that impact our spirit/soul in a positive way, directly or indirectly. These healthy habits will not only affect our spirit/soul positively, but impact the non-tangible, but very real, parts of our life such as our relationships with others and our eternal destination. We will now delve into a few more areas where developing healthy life habits will demonstrate the full impact to all parts of our being.

The second healthy life habit that will be addressed is effectively managing the resources God has provided. For this discussion the use of the term resources will be limited to our finances or money. Too often the only attention most people give to managing their resources is when they are pressured to do so. In this case, the management of resources would be reactionary. For example, resources are acted upon when a notification is received that a payment is overdue on a particular bill. A person may be in a constant mode of scrambling to pay bills. This will generate much stress. The stress will be unhealthy for our physical bodies. The stress may also cause us to abandon other healthy life habits we developed or are working to develop. For example, financial stress could lead us to frequently eat "emotional comfort food", which may interfere with our efforts to become or maintain physical fitness. So, you can quickly see that some unhealthy life habits will influence the ability to develop healthy life habits in other areas of our lives.

What are the healthy life habits with regard to managing our resources and how do we develop them? There are many books written on this subject by some very knowledgeable people. Sometimes the enormous amount of information available regarding managing our resources is viewed as overwhelming. The task of sifting through the information to arrive at the answers that can be applied to our lives is often viewed as daunting. Fortunately, God gives us the answers. We just need to listen to what He says and do as He has instructed us. It is important to know what God says about how we should manage our resources. First, how do we obtain resources? In the book of Proverbs, chapter 10, verse 4, God tells us, "Lazy hands make a man poor, but diligent hands bring wealth." In the same book, chapter 21, verse 5, God says, "The plans of the diligent lead to profit." The book of Proverbs is full of wisdom. Many of the scriptures throughout the Bible can be viewed as promises from God and principles we can live by. The book of Proverbs is no exception. These two verses emphasize the importance of hard work and the importance of planning ahead. The definition of hard work varies from person to person. However, God's definition does not change. He expects us to work hard six days each week. The bottom line here is that hard work will lead to an abundance of resources. Many people believe they are being diligent but have misunderstood the full concept. Diligence is defined as "the careful and persistent work or effort." So, there are two elements. There is the one most people think of, which is persistent work or effort. Someone may say that they work full-time and sometimes overtime at a job. That would certainly qualify as persistent work or effort. However, the other element, "careful", is equally important. For example, think about two employees who perform the same job. Both employees are very loyal in terms of coming to work every day. The difference is that one of the employees does just enough to meet the minimum requirements of the job and the other employee always does more than is expected. The latter employee is fulfilling the "careful" element of the diligence definition. Now, let's further assume that a position becomes available which would be a promotion for either of the two employees in our hypothetical example. It is fair to assume the employee who consistently did more than expected would be chosen to be promoted to the open position. So, by being diligent, the employee who was promoted was, in fact, managing his/her resources effectively. This diligence is certainly a healthy life habit.

The term "careful" in the definition of diligence also means thorough. You have likely heard the expressions, "Don't leave any stone unturned" or "Make sure you dot every i and cross every t." These expressions relate to how thorough a person is. In whatever we do in life, we are to be thorough. If you need some motivation, God tells us in Colossians, chapter 3, verses 23-24, "Whatever you do, work at it with all your heart, as working for the Lord, not for human masters, since you know that you will receive an inheritance from the Lord as a reward. It is the Lord Christ you are serving." Think about that, even though we may have a human boss at our job on earth, our attitude and drive to do the best should come from the knowledge that our God is our ultimate authority and the one we are serving. Because we love Him, we want to serve Him. And, when we serve Him with "all our heart" (maximum effort), He will reward us. These rewards transcend time. Some will be realized during our time on earth and some will be eternal. The eternal rewards are worth much more than our earthly rewards. That sounds like something every human should be interested in and motivated by. The rewards are another promise from God. We would be wise to take Him up on every one of His promises. Once we understand the rewards God has for us, we should want to do everything in our power to achieve those rewards. Everything in our power just means doing what God says **and** letting Him work through us. For example, if you are a teacher and you seek advice from mentor (a trusted friend who is a successful teacher) regarding how you can be the best at what you do, your mentor will guide you, give you tips on what works best and what doesn't work as well. If you focus on what the mentor tells you and put your effort into doing what you were told, you will succeed. In life, God is our mentor. He has told us what works best and what doesn't work. He gives us wisdom that can be used in every situation we encounter. We just have to listen to Him and do what He says, and do it with every ounce of strength we possess.

How else can we effectively manage our resources? In the book of Proverbs, chapter 11, verse 25, God tells us that, "A generous man will prosper; he who refreshed others will himself be refreshed." In the book of Proverbs, chapter 25, verse 9 God says, "A generous man will himself be blessed, for he shares his food with the poor." Helping those in need is managing our resources effectively. Giving to others on a regular basis is another healthy life habit. We want to be careful not to give because we think we will receive financial resources in return. That would be selfish in nature and God will not reward selfishness. God always examines our hearts, i.e., our motives behind every action. In the book of Proverbs, chapter 5, verse 21 God tells us, "For your ways are in full view of the Lord, and He examines all your paths." Some people fall into the trap of doing good things for the primary purpose of appearance, which is selfish, and not because of God's love moving through them. In the book of Matthew, chapter 6, verse 3, Jesus states, "But when you give to the needy, do not let your left hand know what you right hand is doing, so that your giving may be done in secret." What Jesus is telling us is that giving to help others is very good, however, if we boast about it or go out of our way to make our good deeds known so that we are thought of more highly, our heart is not pure in terms of the giving. We should remain focused on for whom we are doing these good things. If so, the good we do will be motivated by love. Giving out of love for those we give to provides all the benefits we have previously discussed including heavenly rewards. Heavenly blessings from being generous with a pure heart are hard to describe, but we do know they are eternal. God refers to our heavenly rewards as "treasures in Heaven." It is impossible to know precisely what those rewards are unless you have been to Heaven.

Aside from heavenly blessings, there are benefits we enjoy while on earth. The earthly blessings that are received by being generous with a pure heart can be good health (as long as we also take care of our physical body), loving relationships, protection from physical or spiritual harm, and, as we've mentioned at length earlier in this book, joy from serving Him by being a conduit of His love. When you think about it, isn't helping those in need being a conduit of His love?

Another healthy life habit with regard to managing our resources is taking the time to create a personal financial budget. Many people think establishing a budget is too difficult or would not help much. Both thoughts are untrue. The purpose of a budget is to give us a detailed understanding of what needs we have, where our funds are spent, and to have information at our fingertips to use in a proactive manner to make wise decisions that will affect our financial ability for many years into the future. Having the willpower to adhere to the budget will enable us to reap the rewards in the long run. Many people do not realize that short-term sacrifices lead to long-term benefits that far outweigh those sacrifices. For example, a person may think that saving $5 per week will not help much. However, if we save $5 per week and that $5 is invested conservatively and earns 6% per year, we will have over $20,000 after 30 years. If we save $50 per week for the same period of time, we would have over $200,000 at the end of the time period. Therefore, because of compound interest and consistent saving, you really can have a nice sum of money to supplement your income when the time comes for you to enjoy retirement. It just takes a little sacrifice and some diligence now.

Here are the key factors to consider when creating a budget. Each of us that has a certain amount of income knows what that amount of income is likely to be weekly, biweekly, or monthly. So, we begin with that amount of income. Then we list every expense we incur and estimate the amount of each particular expense for the next 12 months based upon history and other facts we know. Examples of spending are utility expenses (electricity, cell phone, water/sewer, cable TV, WiFi, garbage pickup), gasoline for our vehicles, insurance (for our vehicles and other property or our own lives), donations, clothes, food, entertainment, vacation fund, a payment on a automobile loan, a mortgage payment, vehicle or other equipment repairs, minor maintenance at our homes, property taxes, work expenses, and you can probably think of a few more. Simply subtract the expenses from the income for each month. Whatever is left over, plan to put a portion of it into a savings account. If there is nothing left over, effort must be put into determining how to reduce expenses or increase income. That's budgeting 101 in a paragraph. The more diligent and disciplined we are in establishing and monitoring a budget, the greater chance we will have success in managing our resources, or better put, managing the resources God has provided.

We could easily devote an entire chapter of this book to managing our resources, but that is not our sole focus. There is one last thought that we want to convey to encourage you before moving on to the next healthy life habit. Please know that each of us can acquire unhealthy life habits regarding managing our resources very easily. No one should be overly critical of themselves for the development of unhealthy life habits, whether those habits are management of resources based or in another area of our lives, but we should take small steps toward building healthy life habits. The ultimate motivation is to do something to please God. By doing so, we reap benefits now and throughout eternity.

The third healthy life habit to be discussed is developing patience. We all are subjected to external influences that try our patience. If we are running just a few minutes late for work, or to go see a movie, or church, it is likely we will become impatient if we encounter a slow moving vehicle on the road. The level of impatience grows if the circumstances are more serious, for example, if a woman is in labor and rushing to the hospital or a person was seriously injured and hurrying to the emergency room. The latter two examples may seem like the impatience is justified, and, in a way, it certainly is. However, there is a difference between acting with a sense of urgency and acting impatient. A sense of urgency motivates us to move much more quickly than we normally would. We can have a sense of urgency while not showing impatience toward others. Acting with a sense of urgency only means that time is of the essence in our mind. That thinking alone does not make us demonstrate impatience toward other people. Impatience toward others means they have done something that we don't like and we become irritated with them. Not only can we have a sense of urgency and not become impatient toward others, but the opposite is also possible. We may not have a sense of urgency regarding current circumstances, but become impatient with other people. An example of the latter follows. Let's assume you are busy working on a project and your young child walks up to you and asks you a question. You ignore the child's question initially, but the child asks again and continues to do so until you answer. Because you are more concerned about your project than the child's question, you become impatient toward the child. Can you see that this behavior is rooted in thinking of oneself more than others (in this case, the child)? For another example, let's assume you live with several family members. One of the family members never makes their bed or helps clean the dishes or leaves the shower curtain open after showering or......on and on. Our response toward this family member, if not rooted in love, will likely be impatience. The basis for the impatience is selfishness. What can overcome selfishness? Agape love working through us.

It is not practical to think we can avoid situations that would lead to impatience. It is wise to prepare ourselves to respond in love when we are tempted to be impatient with someone. What steps can we take to prepare ourselves to respond in love? We must practice thinking of others more than ourselves every day. That does not come naturally for us, but the more we do it, the more we realize the benefits of loving others and thinking of the needs of others before thinking of ourselves. We have many opportunities to practice patience every day. When we think of others needs before our own desires, we are ensuring that we are loving the person with God's love. This may sound repetitive, but we must stay focused at all times on how much love we show another human being, regardless of the natural tendencies to think of our own needs first. This is not an easy task on our own, but with God's help, we can develop a consistent flow of love through us to others.

A second way we can prepare ourselves to respond to people in love rather than impatience is by gaining wisdom. In the book of Proverbs, chapter 19, verse 11 God says, "A man's wisdom gives him patience." The Hebrew word sekel, used here for the word wisdom in this verse, means great intelligence and good sense. Wisdom is gained from understanding the truth. Understanding the truth is a goal of this book. Wisdom comes from God because God knows all. He loves us and wants us to gain wisdom by understanding the truth. He tells us that if we listen to Him, we will know the truth, and the truth will set us free. There is a passage in the book of John, chapter 8, verses 31-36 when Jesus is having a conversation with some folks who believe the fact that He is God. In this passage Jesus reiterates what I just mentioned about gaining truth and, because we understand the truth, we gain freedom. What are we gaining freedom from? We are gaining freedom from sin. You can easily make the case that impatience is sin because we are allowing our impatience to interfere with God's command to love the person with whom we are being impatient. Therefore, if we gain freedom from sin by acquiring wisdom, we could also say that we can gain freedom from being impatient by acquiring wisdom. Let's see how this works. If someone is driving very slowly in the left lane of a major highway, traveling significantly below the speed limit, and we are behind the person driving slowly, we may be tempted to become impatient with the driver of the slow vehicle. If we learn that the person driving slowly in front of us was in the midst of experiencing a stroke or heart attack, we would quickly change our perspective and, instead of being impatient with the person, we would call for help for that person. Learning about the truth, understanding the truth, and applying the truth to every situation we encounter is wisdom. This wisdom has the ability to guide our actions in a powerful manner. God knows it and He is trying to get all of humanity to understand this spiritual principle. As you consider many situations that occur in your life when you are tempted to become impatient, you will find those temptations will diminish when you gain understanding regarding what is causing the person you are tempted to become impatient with to behave in a certain manner. If someone is driving a bit recklessly and you are not happy with their driving, you will tend to become impatient or even angry with the driver. However, what if you discover that the person is driving his pregnant wife to the hospital because she is about to deliver a baby.

That fact may justify his erratic driving behavior, but whether it does or not, that fact does warrant us having more patience with the other driver. The challenge for us is that we may never learn what is causing a particular behavior by another person. It is during these circumstances where patience, motivated by love, must be given based upon an internal acknowledgment that the individual who is behaving in a manner that will cause us to be tempted to become impatient has no malicious intent. That thought will usually diffuse any potential occurrence for animosity between you and the other person. We should always, therefore, assume the other person is not doing something intentionally to offend us or make us angry. That line of thinking will enable us to be patient with all other people. In fact, if we assume there is no malicious intent but there really is malicious intent, we will show the other person patience and compassion because we are thinking positively of the other person's motives. The book of Zechariah, chapter 7, verses 9-10, God tells us, "This is what the Lord Almighty says: Administer true justice; show mercy and compassion to one another. Do not oppress the widow or the fatherless, the alien or the poor. In your hearts do not think evil of each other." Expressing compassion by not condemning (which is thinking evil of another person) the actions of others, even if they have wrong motives, is an act of love. The reason we can show patience, regardless of the other person's motives, is that our reaction is based upon loving the person rather than judging the person.

Another important reason not to judge is that not one of us is perfect. In the book of Luke, chapter 6, verse 41, Jesus says, "Why do you look at the speck of sawdust in your brother's eye and pay no attention to the plank in your own eye?" What Jesus is telling us is that no human being is perfect, or without fault. So, why are we so quick to be critical or unforgiving or impatient with others when we may do things that are equally worthy of criticism. Many people enjoy going out to eat. If you go to a restaurant, place an order, and the food you are served is not what you ordered, you may be tempted to become impatient with the server. The server may have made an honest mistake. There was clearly no malicious intent. In other words, the server did not want to place an inaccurate order to the cook, but some may be quick to condemn the actions of the server. Furthermore, the server may have placed the order accurately to the cook and the cook made a mistake. The cook did not intend to make the mistake, but some may fall to the temptation to show impatience with the server when an honest mistake was made by the cook. This is where the application of wisdom always leads us to respond in an appropriate manner. Wisdom, in this case, is understanding that people are not perfect and will occasionally make a mistake. Knowing that fact, which we can clearly attest to given the mistakes we have made in our own lives, should influence our ability to respond to the server in a patient manner. In addition, if we approach every interaction with others by loving them, our response will reflect that love. The combination of knowledge that people are imperfect and showing love toward others, when applied, is an example of wisdom in action.

What should our behavior be when we become impatient with ourselves, or impatient regarding something that is not happening fast enough in our lives? As always, God gives us great guidance and advice. In the book of Romans, chapter 8, verse 25, God tells us, "But if we hope for what we do not yet have, we wait for it patiently." The key words are hope and patience. There is no doubt hope provides patience. To illustrate this concept, let's assume you have a goal of earning a college degree. It is a known fact that you must work hard for the degree. It will likely take 3-5 years of attending classes, studying, and being diligent in your efforts. These requirements will impose demands on your time in addition to any other responsibilities you have in life. During the time you are going to college, the amount of work required of you may discourage you along the way. That discouragement may lead you to think that obtaining a college degree is not worth the effort. If you convince yourself that the effort is too much for the desired outcome, you will soon become less motivated to finish your coursework and earn the college degree. In essence, the hope you held for obtaining a college degree subsided or vanished completely. However, if you are focused on the goal and believe that obtaining the college degree is worth the effort, and whatever sacrifice is needed to ensure the goal is achieved, you will continue to be motivated to achieve the goal and your hope will be a source of patience during your pursuit of a college degree.

The concept of hope giving us patience applies to goals we create for ourselves in almost any area of our lives. The more difficult the road traveled to achieve a particular goal, the more easily we can develop unwavering hope. The logic here begins with the fact that there are only two possibilities when pursuing a difficult goal. The first is that we will work hard and achieve the goal. The second is that we will abandon our efforts and discontinue pursuing the goal. For the former, the process of achieving the goal comes from an internal motivation fueled by hope. The hope comes from believing that achieving the goal will improve our lives and that we have the ability to successfully achieve the goal. In the book of Romans, chapter 5, verses 3-4 God tells us, "that suffering produces perseverance; perseverance, character; and character, hope." Therefore, if you stay focused on a specific goal, and that goal is not easily achievable, there will be a natural inclination to have our hope strengthened as we make progress toward achieving the goal. The strengthening of our hope comes from the character we develop because we persevere.

We will be patient with ourselves because of the realization that we are pursuing goals that are good for us, some of these goals may be difficult to achieve, and some of these goals may take a long period of time to achieve. Patience with ourselves will be manifested by daily self-encouragement, i.e. when we are patient with ourselves we will be our best source of encouragement. This creates a very positive mindset and provides energy and drive to achieve. On the other hand, if we are impatient with ourselves, we will be critical of our behavior. This will lead to becoming discouraged, creating a negative mindset, which in the extreme, will become depression and can have very bad consequences. The difference between encouraging ourselves and discouraging ourselves has enormous ramifications during our life on earth and for eternity. If we believe in God, and God's love has been placed into our hearts through His Holy Spirit, we have the means to always be an encourager, both to ourselves and others. In the book of Romans, chapter 5, verse 5, God says, "And hope does not put us to shame, because God's love has been poured out into our hearts through the Holy Spirit, Who has been given to us." Therefore, we will encourage ourselves and not discourage ourselves because of the love of God flowing through us. It is not unholy to love ourselves. It is holy. God loves us (much scripture on this subject; the book of John, chapter 17, verse 23 is one example) and desires for His love to be the embodiment of what influences how we act, even toward ourselves. Through this analysis of patience with ourselves, it should be apparent that patience with ourselves is loving ourselves. Just as patience with others is loving others.

You may think that much of what you have read thus far in this book seems to, at some point, circle back to love. When it comes to human behavior, Agape love is the force that enables us to maximize what God can accomplish through us during our time on earth. In fact, without Agape love working through us, none of our earthly accomplishments mean anything in terms of eternal ramifications. Look what God tells us in the book of I Corinthians, chapter 13, verse 3. He says, "If I give all I possess to the poor and give over my body to hardship that I may boast, but do not have love, I gain nothing." God wants our hearts filled with His love because He knows the tremendous benefits to the human race. To further drive home the point, in the same book of the Bible and chapter, in verse 13, God says, "And now these three remain; faith, hope, and love. But the greatest of these is love."

As chapter 6 of this book comes to a close, please be reminded that throughout the discussion of building healthy life habits just a few key areas in life were touched upon. The concepts behind building every healthy life habit can, and should, be applied to all areas of our lives. All that is needed to successfully build healthy life habits is the desire, effort, and most of all, Agape love.

CHAPTER 7

Secular Thought vs. Spiritual Thought

There are many forces that work against us as we seek to develop strong, healthy life habits and to seek understanding of the many physical and spiritual truths. In chapter 2, we've discussed spiritual forces that work against us and those that work for us. These spiritual forces are not typically visible. What about the physical dimension? What forces work against us that exist in the dimension we can see? Furthermore, once those forces are identified, what can be done to extinguish the influence of those forces in our life?

First, let's define what is meant by a force that works against us that cannot be seen. In the spiritual realm, we may have knowledge that the forces we discussed in chapter 2 exist, as God has revealed knowledge of those forces to us, but we may never physically see them. To believe in what is not seen is the fundamental foundation of faith.

In the physical realm, however, when we obtain knowledge that certain things exist, we can typically conclusively identify the specific items. We can prove the existence of something we learn about that exists in the physical realm and, thereby, provide clarity to others through a variety of means. For example, if you visit the Grand Canyon in the United States in the State of Arizona and return home, you can describe the Grand Canyon to a friend or family member who did not accompany you on your visit. Not only can you describe it, but you could likely show your friend or family member pictures you took while visiting. In the physical dimension, proving something exists is usually relatively easy. The easiest way to prove something exists is visually. However, you could prove something exists by utilizing other senses as well. Let's assume you live in a rural area and you hear a woodpecker knocking on a tree occasionally. If you record the sound of a woodpecker knocking on a tree you will have sound to support your claim that you know there is a woodpecker near where you live. In this case, the truth is verified through the sense of hearing. As a final example we will tap into the sense of taste. If new restaurant opens in the town where you live and someone tells you that the restaurant is thought to have the best tasting pizza, a simple trip to the restaurant for lunch or dinner will confirm what you heard by using your sense of taste. In the physical dimension, there is always a means to prove, or disprove, a truth. The only thing that prevents people from finding physical truths is not digging deep enough, i.e., not asking enough questions and capturing facts that will lead to a complete understanding of the truth. God implores us in the book of Proverbs, chapter 23, verse 23 to "Buy the truth and do not sell it; get wisdom, discipline and understanding." What God is saying is that if our desire for something is strong enough, we will search for what it is we are desiring, and when we find it, we will obtain it. Once we have possession of whatever it is that we desire, we should not let it go for any price. He is also telling us that we should have a strong desire for the truth, and seek it fervently. Then, after we have obtained the truth, we should not give it up easily and, in fact, never give it up. In other words, once we have a truth, there is never a reason to relinquish that truth inasmuch as there is nothing as valuable to us as the truth. The impact of knowing the truth and using the truth in our lives is always positive. Knowing the truth is called understanding. Applying the truth in our lives is called wisdom.

God has given us spiritual truths to apply even as we live in a physical world. He knows we will learn about physical truths over time since we live on earth in the physical realm. However, spiritual truths are impossible for us to know without divine revelation. God, of course, knows that spiritual truths are not only beyond our ability to know without His help, but He has taken on the task of explaining spiritual truths to people who live in a physical world. That is not an easy task from a human's perspective. However, from God's perspective, communicating spiritual truths to us is probably as effortless for Him as us telling someone our own name. Furthermore, since God knows that it is much harder for us to comprehend spiritual truths, He helps us by revealing spiritual truths through His Word, repeating the truths often, using many analogies, and chronicling history with the exact detail to teach us exactly what His deepest truths mean. We have talked about many spiritual truths in this book. Knowing and understanding spiritual truths will not only help us every day we spend on earth, but is essential for achieving success that is everlasting.

The purpose of this chapter is to examine the difference between secular thought (which is largely culture driven) and spiritual thought (the genesis of which is God), as well as understand how each type of thought affects our ability to see God's truths. We add the term independent to spiritual thought to emphasize that a person is not influenced by secular thinking when thinking independently about spiritual matters.

Both physical and spiritual truths are more easily understood if we think independently rather than allowing the culture we live in define these truths for us. Thinking independently is vital to knowing the truth. Thinking independently doesn't guarantee we will understand the truth. Why? Because we may make assumptions before fully pursuing facts. In other words, we can think independently and still draw incorrect conclusions based upon assumptions. If we think independently while pursuing facts it is highly probable that we will come to know a truth. This applies to physical and spiritual truths. On the other hand, if we allow the culture to define spiritual truth we will undoubtedly not know a spiritual truth because the culture is largely secular minded. This is, obviously, very dangerous to a society inasmuch as the lack of knowledge of a spiritual truth will lead to immorality. The reason is the spiritual truths that have been rejected or distorted by a purely secular thinking society means the society will function without a set of moral guidelines to follow. Secular thinking is thinking that is void of a spiritual basis. It is, therefore, impossible to understand and gain knowledge about a spiritual truth if your thinking is secular based.

If we allow the culture to define a physical truth for us, the culture's secular foundational thinking may or may not hinder our understanding of the reality of a particular physical truth. The reason is secular thinking generally is not biased when evaluating physical truths, however, the person who has a secular worldview is still a fallible human being and, hence, can make mistakes by drawing incorrect conclusions about physical truths. Those incorrect conclusions are easily clarified and corrected if the person who made the mistake remains open minded and listens to additional facts. Some physical truths are difficult to prove or disprove. Sometimes, we can use spiritual truths to prove or disprove inaccurate perceptions of physical truths. For example, there are many who believe that when a woman becomes pregnant the cells in her womb have not yet become a human being so removing those cells is an option without a moral dilemma. However, God tells us in Psalm chapter 139, verse 13, "For you created my inmost being; you knit me together in my mother's womb." If we believe the spiritual truth in the book of Psalms, we would conclude that what is believed by many to be a physical truth about life in the womb is incorrect. This subject will be revisited shortly.

Any thought generated by any person has the potential to be incorrect, or miss the truth. Every thought that is not in sync with truth, whether the subject matter is a physical truth or spiritual truth, is an erroneous thought.

Please review the following statements that illustrate the connections between the two types of thinking and the two types of truths.

Secular Thinking About Physical Truth -------> Can Lead to Understanding the Truth

Secular Thinking About Spiritual Truth -------> Will Not Find and Understand the Truth

Independent Spiritual Thinking About Physical Truth -----> May Lead to Understanding the Truth

Independent Spiritual Thinking About Spiritual Truth -----> Will Likely Lead to Understanding the Truth

If we seek to understand a spiritual truth, the act of seeking will typically be accompanied by independent spiritual thought. Likewise, if we seek to understand a physical truth, the act of seeking will typically be accompanied by secular based thought. The latter is not always the case.

You could use independent spiritual thinking to explain a physical truth. You could use the analogy of language to drive home these points. If a person decides to learn the Chinese language, they must use a very different alphabet than the English language uses. Secular thought used in pursuit of understanding physical truths is using the Chinese alphabet to learn the Chinese language. Similarly, independent spiritual thought used in pursuit of understanding spiritual truths is like using the English alphabet to learn the English language. In both cases the alphabet is the tool, and a vital tool, to accomplishing the person's goal. There is one exception. You can use independent spiritual thought to bring about understanding of some physical truths. For example, while we are enjoying life on earth we occupy a physical body. Secular thinking will confirm for us that the physical body we occupy will expire someday. Independent spiritual thinking also confirms for us that the physical body we occupy will expire someday. In the book of Hebrews, chapter 9, verse 27 God tells us that, "it is appointed unto men once to die." This death is physical death. Thinking about this verse gives us assurance, or confirmation, that we can expect, with certainty, our physical bodies will perish.

As you review the four statements of thinking and truths above, please notice that the strongest relationship between thinking and understanding the truth is independent spiritual thinking and spiritual truth.

To fully understand a physical or spiritual truth, much effort must be exerted. Generally, the greater the effort, the deeper our understanding of the truth. Assuming effort is given, when we think spiritually we have a mindset that is conducive to understanding. That is not to say that when we think in secular ways, we do not have a mindset that is conducive to understanding, but rather that secular thinking is influenced by cultural waves of thought, which are more likely to interfere with understanding a truth. These waves of thought may be accurate or may not be accurate. There is a natural force associated with secular thinking that results in a pull toward accepting the beliefs of a society, or subset of individuals in that society. In other words, taking on the secular thought of someone or a group of people seems to be a common occurrence, particularly if that thinking becomes widespread within society. When we think with independent spiritual thought, if we are diligent we will find the spiritual truth, regardless of what society or others believe. That may sound a bit confusing but remember there is only one truth for any given subject matter. We are more inclined to find the truth if that truth is a spiritual truth than if the truth is a physical truth when we use the right type of thinking. Some will debate this point by saying that there are many who will say they understand a spiritual truth, but their belief is inaccurate. Therefore, the person's lack of understanding of a spiritual truth is evidence that independent spiritual thinking does not always guarantee understanding spiritual truth. That is obviously correct as not every spiritual belief system has an accurate view of some, or any, spiritual truths. If you refer back to the fourth statement of thinking and truth the term "likely" is used to describe whether or not someone thinking with independent spiritual thought will understand a spiritual truth. What prevents some people with the right thinking mindset of independent spiritual thinking from understanding the spiritual truth in this case are human emotion and a mix of secular thinking with independent spiritual thinking. The result is untruth being presented as truth. These untruths may seem to make sense logically and be appealing to some, but they are still untruths. Furthermore, you could drop the word "independent" from the description of spiritual thinking in these cases as this type of spiritual thinking is not independent of secular thinking.

How do we ensure that our pursuit of spiritual truth is not influenced by secular thought? There are two strategies for avoiding the undesired intrusion of secular thought when in pursuit of spiritual truth. The first strategy to ensuring secular thought does not interfere with our understanding of a spiritual truth is to keep our minds focused on spiritual thinking and avoiding secular thinking when pursuing a spiritual matter. That sounds obvious, but our enemy will attempt to distract us continuously. The support for the first strategy is found in the book of Romans, chapter 12, verse 2, which reads, "Do not conform to the pattern of this world, but be transformed by the renewing of your mind. Then you will be able to test and approve what God's will is-His good, pleasing and perfect will." We will discuss the second sentence of this verse first. God's perfect will is simply accomplished when we align our thoughts and actions with what He intended. He desires for us to love Him completely and to love others by allowing His power, Agape love, to flow through us. When we contemplate information to determine whether or not we have found a spiritual truth, we are, in fact, testing the information for its authenticity. If the information we encounter is contradictory in some way to God's will, you can be assured that you have not found a spiritual truth. Conversely, if the information you come across is consistent with God's will, you can be confident you are on the right track to learning a spiritual truth. In the first strategy, which is revealed in the first sentence of the verse in Romans we have quoted, we find the following to be true. To see spiritual truth clearly, we must transform our thinking (the renewing of our mind) by eliminating secular thought during those times when we are attempting to understand a spiritual truth. That is not to say that we must eliminate secular thought completely, but eliminate secular thought when thinking about spiritual truths. Secular thought will act as mental smoke screen that will inhibit our ability to comprehend the spiritual truth. When we transform our thinking and eliminate secular thought, spiritual truths become clear. The verse in Romans goes a bit further by emphatically instructing us not to conform our behavior to what occurs naturally in the world. That means we should conform our behavior to God's will, and not what secular minded thinking deems is appropriate. There are many examples that can be given to demonstrate this concept. One of the subjects that will raise emotions quickly and be debated fiercely is abortion. From a purely secular point of view, there is no God telling the secular minded person that taking the life of an unborn child is just as much murder as committing the same act a day after birth. Thinking about this issue from a spiritually minded perspective will produce a conclusion that all life was created by God, that all life is precious, that all life should be protected (God also tells us directly to protect the innocent...I doubt a person can be more innocent than while still in his/her mother's womb), and that terminating life is murder. Secular thinking will introduce thoughts such as, "What about the rights a mother has to control what happens to her body?", or "The child would have a terrible life if born as the biological parents have no means to provide for the child", or "The doctors are telling me there is a 50% chance this child may have a birth defect of some kind." Spiritual truth regarding abortion is clear. Secular thinking about abortion will interfere with understanding the spiritual truth. An absence of understanding the spiritual truth about abortion will lead to behavior that is not consistent with God's will. Although it is not the purpose of this book to debate the subject of abortion, one of the purposes of this book is to show how to get to the truths of life that will enhance the joy you experience during your time on earth, and beyond that enable you to enjoy life with God forever. Thinking clearly about spiritual truths is how you maximize your joy now and forever.

The second strategy to minimizing or eliminating the effect of secular thought in our thinking when pursuing a spiritual truth is tangent to the first, but highlights how clearly secular and spiritual thinking differ. The text to support the second strategy is found in the book of Colossians, chapter 2, verse 8, which reads, "See to it that no one takes you captive through hollow and deceptive philosophy, which depends on human tradition and the elemental spiritual forces of this world rather than on Christ." The second strategy is simple. Remain focused on the revelations God has given us in His Word inasmuch as Jesus Christ is the Word and, therefore, you will be able to subdue the spiritual forces of this world. We will work through this scripture from the beginning, and amplify with other scripture to provide a thorough understanding. You have progressed far enough into this book to know that in the spiritual dimension there is an ongoing battle. This battle, of course, is between good and evil. When opposing forces go to battle, there is usually a very good reason. In this case, the reason for battle is that both sides are attempting to capture your soul (your mind). One side is doing it through what God refers to in this verse in the book of Colossians as hollow and deceptive philosophy. Hollow refers to the emptiness of the thought or pattern of thoughts that compose a theory. Deceptive refers to the fact that the purported truths supported by this theory of hollow thinking are, in fact, lies. Where do the lies originate? This is taught clearly in the book of John, chapter 8, verses 42-44, which reads, "Jesus said to them, 'If God were your Father, you would love me, for I have come here from God. I have not come on my own; God sent me. Why is my language not clear to you? Because you are unable to hear what I say. You belong to your father, the devil, and you want to carry out your father's desires. He was a murderer from the beginning, not holding to the truth, for there is no truth in him. When he lies, he speaks his native language, for he is a liar and the father of lies." Keep in mind that Jesus is speaking to a group of people who are already deceived. The author and originator of the lies is none other than Satan himself. He hates God and hates us. The people Jesus is speaking to not only have believed the lies, but have a passion for carrying out actions that the lies dictate. The danger for those who believe the lies is that their actions are carried out in accordance with the lies and in outright opposition to a spiritual truth. The second part of the verse in Colossians acknowledges the fact that the hollow and deceptive philosophy that comes our way is delivered in a package of human tradition and elemental spiritual forces of this world. The elemental spiritual forces of this world refers to Satan and his tactics. Another strong force is human tradition. Human tradition can be a force for good or a force for evil. For example, in the United States of America we gather together with family and friends every fourth Thursday in November to give thanks to God for what we have been given. It has become a tradition for us in America.

We call this time Thanksgiving. What we do on Thanksgiving is a force for good. However, the verse in Colossians is warning us of how human tradition can be a force for evil. Halloween is a good example of a tradition in the United States of America that is a force for evil. Not everyone who participates in Halloween is evil or doing anything evil, however, many who do participate in Halloween are celebrating witchcraft, death, and ill will toward others. There is no connection with God our Father while you are focusing on witches, vampires, ghosts, and the devil. Hence, it is safe to assume that you will not uncover any spiritual truths while letting your mind dwell upon the evil things associated with Halloween. As a side note, please be encouraged to research the origins of Halloween. You will be enlightened and most likely think twice about your approach to this "holiday" the next time the end of October rolls around.

In this chapter we have discussed the two primary types of thinking and the two types of truths that exist. The importance of recognizing secular thought cannot be overemphasized. The more adept a person is at identifying secular thought, the more successful that person will be in his/her pursuit of spiritual truth. How do we identify secular thought? In the book of Psalms, chapter 10, verse 4, God tells us, "In his pride the wicked does not seek him; in all his thoughts there is no room for God." Secular thought is the absence of thought about God. In fact, a purely secular thinker will likely either classify themselves as agnostic or atheistic in terms of their worldview. When you listen or read something espoused by a solely secular thinking person, you will notice the absence of God and the truths of God in their thinking. For example, a secular minded person may believe that when their physical body dies that is the end of all there is to their existence. Since you know that the absence of God in thought is secular, you can quickly identify the previous sentence as a secular point of view. As you pursue spiritual truth about God, you will ignore the secular thought, in this case, the idea that your physical body being all there is to your existence. But, to ignore secular thought you must recognize it.

Let's look at an example of secular thought that is less obvious. You are having a discussion over lunch with a coworker. You and your coworker are talking about the environment, specifically, taking care of planet Earth. Your coworker agrees with you that people should not litter on land or in waterways such as lakes, rivers, and oceans. You both further agree that we should do all that is possible to maintain clean air and that we should replenish forests as we cut down trees to make lumber. How would you detect a secular worldview that is prevalent in your coworker's thinking? Thinking back about the conversation, you recall a statement you made giving credit to God for the amazing creation that He literally spoke into existence and that we owe it to Him to care for His creation. Your coworker, in response to you, said, "Yes, we should respect mother earth since it is the home of the human race." The intentional exclusion of God by your coworker is the key to determining that the thinking of your coworker is secular.

Identifying secular thought is vital to preventing it from influencing your thought as you pursue spiritual truth. Consistently identifying secular thought and successfully preventing it from influencing your spiritual thought as you pursue spiritual truth will make focusing on spiritual truth through spiritual thought much easier. In addition, when you have developed a strong habit of thinking spiritually, it becomes much easier to ignore secular thought. This is not simply a matter of deciding which thought you desire (secular or spiritual) and thinking a certain way. In its infancy, this is a matter of pursuing spiritual truth with a constant focus on answering the most fundamental spiritual question, "Who is God?" As you recall, a discussion of who God is took place early in this book. Please know that the fullness of God cannot be taught or explained in any one book. However, some of the most important elements of God (from what He has revealed to us) have been discussed in the first three chapters of this book. As long as you prevent secular thought from influencing your thinking, the nature of God never really ceases to be understood by us as it is impossible to think about the subject without digging deeper because you are thinking with a spiritually focused mindset. When we do this, we take small steps toward understanding God more. When we progress past infancy in terms of spiritual thinking by seeking to understand more spiritual truths, we answer questions such as Why did God create us?; What does He expect from us?; and, What is God's will? Those are questions that most people would love to know the answers to and some people spend a lifetime attempting to answer. The truth is God has revealed the answers to these questions to us, and we will discuss some of what God has revealed about these questions in the next chapter.

CHAPTER 8

God's Will

The term "will" is defined as a person's desire or wish for something to be done or carried out. For example, many people prepare a legal document called their "Last Will and Testament."

This document contains instructions for what a person would like to happen when they die. Given there can be no further action desired by the deceased person after the document is read, you would have to agree that the instructions given in the document are certainly the person's last, or final, will.

For those of us who have become parents, we can relate to wanting the best for our children. A parent wants their child to be happy, well provided for, live a morally upstanding life, know God personally, and love God and others. You could say what a parent wants for their child is the parent's will. A parent can raise their child in a manner that will lead to many of the aspects of the parent's will being realized in their child's life. Of course, every child makes their own choices in life. Although those choices may certainly be influenced by how their parents raised them, there are many examples of children who do not follow their parents teaching. That often brings heartache for the parent. When a child chooses a different path than what the parent had hoped for, you could conclude the child did not follow the will of his/her parents. In the same way, we have the ability and freedom to choose to live our lives in conformity to God's will or in rebellion to God's will. For those who live in conformity with God's will, they reap the rewards that God has indicated are to be received for obedience. For those who live in rebellion to God's will, they will be punished in accordance with God's promises regarding rebellion. Just as a parent is pleased when their children follow the parents will, God is pleased when we, as His children, follow His will. We will see that as we explore more deeply His will throughout the rest of this chapter.

You do not have to look any further than when God created us to begin to understand certain elements of God's will. God tells us some of what He asked us to do (His will) upon creating the first man and woman. In the book of Genesis, chapter 1, verses 27-28, we read that "God created man in His own image, in the image of God He created him; male and female He created them. God blessed them and said to them, 'Be fruitful and increase in number; fill the earth and subdue it. Rule over the fish of the sea and the birds of the air and over every living creature that moves on the ground." God asks us to be caretakers of His creation. There is no doubt that God intended for us to have dominion over every other non-human living thing. He clearly communicates our purpose, which is to populate the earth while also caring for every part of this planet. These actions are part of God's will for us. There is much more to God's will for us than to procreate and take care of His creation, not to diminish the importance of those commands in the least.

God's will is multi-faceted. It is like a diamond in the sense that there are many sides to God's will and the entirety of His will for us is both beautiful and of great value. Unlike our earthly parents' will, God's will is perfect because He is perfect. As earnest and pure as an earthly parent's will may be, it does not compare to the will of an all loving, infinite, and perfect God. Why would we doubt the will of our Heavenly Father who created us? If we believe in God as our Heavenly Father, creator of the universe, and an infinite being, we would not doubt His will. However, if we diminish in our minds, to any degree, who God is, or worse yet, deny the existence of God, that certainly could lead a person to doubting God's will in part or entirely. There is obvious danger in doubting God's will as the ramifications of disobedience are not just severe, but catastrophic and eternal. Conversely, the rewards associated with carrying out God's will in our lives are largely beyond comprehension, but we do know those rewards will exceed anything we know of or can experience now. In addition, we know the rewards for carrying out God's will are eternal. There are many references to be cited to support this, but we will cite only four. In the book of Ephesians, chapter 6, verse 7 and part of verse 8, God tells us to, "Serve wholeheartedly, as if you were serving the Lord, not men, because you know that the Lord will reward everyone for whatever good he does." In the book of Colossians, chapter 3, verses 23-24, God tells us, "Whatever you do, work at it with all your heart, as working for the Lord, not for men, since you know that you will receive an inheritance from the Lord as a reward. It is the Lord Christ you are serving." Please notice a couple of important points in these two scripture citations. First, both contain the concept of "serving". When you serve someone, you are submitting to their will. Therefore, if you humbly submit to God, it will be easier to carry out His will. Secondly, both verses contain the concept of a "reward". We know the reward God promised is eternal life. To support this fact, two more scripture references will be cited. The third scripture is from the book of Romans, chapter 6, verse 23. God tells us, "For the wages of sin is death, but the gift of God is eternal life in Christ Jesus our Lord."

The fourth scripture is from the book of Romans, chapter 2, verse 7, where God tells us, "To those who by persistence in doing good seek glory, honor and immortality, He will give eternal life." The third and fourth scriptures clearly confirm that our reward is eternal life. Who wouldn't want eternal life? This is somewhat rhetorical as everyone would want eternal life. The sad fact is some do not believe in an eternal condition, or life after our earthly bodies die. However, for those that do believe in some form of existence after our physical bodies die, the only thing that may keep them from eternal life is the deception thrust upon them from our adversary, Satan himself. Chapter 11 will be devoted to exploring the truths about life after physical death.

Let us return to more of the specifics of God's will. In chapter 3, we discussed God's desire for us to love Him and to love others. In chapter 6, scripture was cited that confirmed the fact that God commanded us to love Him and others with all our heart. Both of the commands are obviously God's will. We learned about the importance of fulfilling His will to love Him and to love others. We also learned of the benefits to us of carrying out His will with regard to loving God and others because we are empowered by His love, which is Agape love. If we truly are a conduit of God's love, initiated by our love for Him and extending God's love to others, we are fulfilling His will. Most of the remaining facets of God's will that we will discuss all involve loving God, loving others, or God's love for us.

In the book of 2 Peter, chapter 3, verse 9 God talks about His desire to not want anyone to perish. The verse reads, "The Lord is not slow in keeping His promise, as some understand slowness. Instead He is patient with you, not wanting anyone to perish, but everyone to come to repentance." It is very apparent from this verse that God's will is that no one will perish. The fact that God's will is for all people to repent does not guarantee that all people will repent. He tells us in the book of Matthew, chapter 7, verse 13 that, "wide is the gate and broad is the road that leads to destruction and many enter through it." Therefore, you can clearly see that God does not impose His will on the human race because, if He did, every human would accept salvation. How difficult it must be for God, who loves every human, to know that many will not accept the enormous sacrifice He made on the cross for us. It is not that God is angry at those who do not accept His gift, but that He must have deep sadness knowing some will reject Him and, therefore, will not inherit the kingdom, nor live with God forever. He knows what is best for us but has to let us make choices that may or may not lead to what is best for us. The ramifications are eternal.

Another facet of God's will is that we are baptized after we come to know Jesus Christ as our Lord God. Supporting scripture can be found in multiple places in the Bible, the most common is the book of Mark, chapter 16, verse 16 as God tells us, "Whoever believes and is baptized will be saved, but whoever does not believe will be condemned." When God says something, it is obvious that what He says *is* His will. That is the case with believing and being baptized. He also says that doing both leads to salvation. The belief in Jesus Christ as our Lord carries more weight than baptism, however, baptism is not unimportant. In the same verse that was just cited, you will notice that God tells us whoever does not believe will be condemned. He does not say that whoever is not baptized will be condemned. The book of Luke, chapter 23, verses 32-46, contains a description of the last moments Jesus spent on the cross before His physical body expired. He had brief dialogue with a thief whom was also being crucified, but had a repentant heart. This thief knew who Jesus was and expressed that belief. In response, Jesus told the thief that they would be together in paradise on the very day they spoke to one another. To reiterate, the thief **would be** with Jesus in heaven. The thief had no opportunity to be baptized. Therefore, it is no stretch to conclude that a person's belief in God, rather than baptism, is what enables the person to achieve eternal life with God. However, that is not to say that baptism is unimportant nor discretionary. God still commands us to be baptized. Why would we, loving God for who He is and knowing God asks us to be baptized, willingly choose not be baptized?

How significant is baptism to God? Baptism is so significant to God that Jesus was determined to be baptized as an example for us (Matthew chapter 3, verses 13-17). Being God, Jesus did not need to be baptized, but willingly did so to show us that obedience to God has to be at the forefront of our minds and actions constantly. Having a mindset focused on obedience will motivate us to seek wisdom. As discussed earlier in this book, the accumulation of wisdom will benefit us in every area of our lives. Wisdom will also enable us to be successful in having holy thoughts and acting in a holy manner, which is the definition of walking in righteousness. The act of baptism is symbolic of a spiritual renewal, or cleansing of our sins subsequent to our initial repentance. This spiritual renewal is possible without baptism, however, when we are baptized, we are going beyond just acknowledging Jesus Christ as our Savior. We are putting our faith into action. The act of baptism expresses a deeper commitment to God. This deeper commitment manifests itself in more quickly and effectively developing the mindset described in the previous paragraph. Baptism, accompanied by a deep love for God, will accelerate the process of sanctification. Every time we are obedient to God, the result is always sanctification. Our minds will become renewed and strengthened to avoid sinful behavior.

Another facet of God's will is His desire for us to pursue holiness. We discussed holiness in chapter 3 as we explored Agape love and the nature of God. Whenever holiness is mentioned in the Old Testament, it describes an attribute that God possesses, or better said, an aspect of the nature of God. It is as if the holiness of God being described is unattainable, which is precisely the case. A human being cannot possess holiness as a personal attribute without God. We know that shortly after Jesus Christ came to earth and defeated sin, He returned to Heaven.

When He returned to Heaven, He sent the Holy Spirit to dwell within us. The presence of the Holy Spirit in us enables us to demonstrate holiness in our lives. This occurs because the Holy Spirit speaks to us constantly to remind us of what holy thoughts and behavior are as we process every single thought through our spiritual mind, which is our soul. In the New Testament, when holiness is mentioned, this phenomenon becomes obvious. For example, in the book of Romans, chapter 6, verse 19, God tells us, "I put this in human terms because you are weak in your natural selves. Just as you used to offer the parts of your body in slavery to impurity and to ever-increasing wickedness, so now offer them in slavery to righteousness leading to holiness." In the book of 1 Corinthians, chapter 2, verses 10-14, God summarizes how the Holy Spirit imparts wisdom and truth as follows: "but God has revealed it to us by His Spirit. The Spirit searches all things, even the deep things of God. For who among men knows the thoughts of a man except the man's spirit within him? In the same way no one knows the thoughts of God except the Spirit of God. We have not received the spirit of the world, but the Spirit of who is from God, that we may understand what God has freely given us. This is what we speak, not in words taught us by human wisdom but in words taught by the Spirit, expressing spiritual truths in spiritual words. The man without the Spirit does not accept the things that come from the Spirit of God." We can see from this passage that there is a difference between those who do and do not understand God's truth and wisdom. The difference is those who do have the Holy Spirit within them do understand God's truths. We are privileged to be living in the time subsequent to when God sent His Holy Spirit to be with us. It is unfortunate that many reject the Holy Spirit because they reject God or have hardened their hearts toward God. God wants us to pursue holiness and has provided a way for us to do so.

There are other scripture that corroborate the fact that God wants us to pursue holiness. In the book of Leviticus, chapter 11, verse 45

God says, "I am the Lord, who brought you up out of Egypt to be your God; therefore be holy, because I am holy." And, in the same book, Leviticus, chapter 20, verse 8 God says, "Keep my decrees and follow them. I am the Lord, who makes you holy." In the book of Ezekiel, chapter 36, verse 23, God says, "I will show the holiness of my great name, which has been profaned among the nations, the name you have profaned among them. Then the nations will know that I am the Lord, declares the Sovereign Lord, when I am proved holy through you before their eyes." There are three reasons in these three verses why God wants us to pursue holiness. The first reason is because He is holy. He knows that the more we pursue holiness, the more we pursue Him. The second reason God wants us to pursue holiness is when we pursue holiness, we do so by keeping His decrees, of commands that He makes of us. The third reason God wants us to pursue holiness is so people will know Him and know of His holiness through our holy actions. We come to the realization that when we demonstrate a holy behavior, it is not us, but God working through us to enable the holy behavior. If you are a parent, think of how happy and proud you are when your child makes a wise decision or shows strength in moral character or loves others in humility. You are happy because that behavior your child exhibited in their life will lead to joy and success for them. You are proud because they are your child. In the same way, think of how happy and proud God must feel when we reflect holiness in our thoughts or behavior inasmuch as it is completely because of Him that we are able to think or be holy. Even better than that is fact that God knows others will be drawn to Him because of our holy thoughts or actions. In other words, as He said, people will know Him through us as long as our actions are holy and we are conduits of His love.

God's will is for us to take care of the poor, and to take care of widows and orphans. The following scripture references all contain clear direction to help the poor, widows, and orphans. (James 1:27,

Isaiah 1:17, Ezekiel 34:2-3, Proverbs 28:8, Proverbs 29:7, Job 30:25, Proverbs 28:3, Galatians 2:10, Zechariah 7:10, Jeremiah 5:28, Acts 9:36, 1 Corinthians 13:3, Matthew 19:21, Psalms 15:5, Ezekiel 16:49, Ezekiel 18:17, Deuteronomy 15:7, Isaiah 58:10). Some of these verses also call evil those who neglect or oppress the poor, widows, and orphans. Let's examine just a few of these verses. In the first scripture reference, James 1:27, God tells us that, "Religion that God our Father accepts as pure and faultless is this: to look after orphans and widows in their distress and to keep oneself from being polluted by the world." If you want to please God, you can be assured that helping an orphan or widow when they are in need will do it. Most orphans and widows are innocent victims. If we love all people, there is no extra motivation needed for us to help these who are in need. Another referenced scripture, Isaiah 1:17, has a very similar message; "Learn to do right; seek justice. Defend the oppressed. Take up the cause of the fatherless; plead the case of the widow." Not only should we help the fatherless and widows, but we should make an effort to recruit others to follow our lead. In the book of Proverbs, chapter 28, verse 8, God tells us, "Whoever increases wealth by taking interest or profit from the poor amasses it for another, who will be kind to the poor." God will go as far as taking away wealth from those who take advantage of the poor and give it to those who help the poor. This is consistent with God's promise to reward those who do good, who keep His commands. And, remember, He told us the greatest of the commands is to love God and love your neighbor. If we approach every interaction with love and conform every thought to love, our actions will reflect holiness. This can only be accomplished by knowing God and having constant fellowship with His Holy Spirit. It should be apparent by examining just three of the referenced scripture verses that God's will is to help the poor, widows, and orphans. It should also be apparent that it is His will for two reasons. The first is that He is love and has a deep yearning to help the innocent when in need. The second is that when we help those in need, thereby carrying out His work, we are also being strengthened because of the flow of His love through us. The strength that fills us is from the joy we receive when helping others. The source of the joy is really multidimensional. First, we see the appreciation and happiness of those we are helping. This is not always the case, but appreciation will be evident in a large majority of folks we help. Second, when the motivation for helping is based upon love for those we help, the experience of Agape love flowing through our soul is a joyful event. Third, when we realize that an act of service on our part resulted in real benefit to another person, we feel good about ourselves, specifically, the actions we took. The joy we receive from the third point becomes heightened when we realize that there is not only good that flows through us, but that the source of the good that flows through us is from God. This enlightenment does two things. It helps connect us with God deep within in our minds; and, as we think through the experience (leading to the realization of what God did), our faith is solidified.

You probably realize at this point that all of the thoughts regarding God's will have a common element. That element is Agape love. In other words, every aspect of God's will is rooted in Agape love. When you think about it, how could any aspect of God's will not be rooted in Agape love when we know that He is Agape love? There are few truths presented in this book that have the potential to change a person's life more than the understanding of what God's will is, the genesis of His will, and how we can achieve His will with His Agape love working through us. When we firmly grasp this concept, we begin to shift our perspective as we evaluate future situations that we encounter in life. This perspective shift alters how we react to every interaction in life in as much as we view each situation through the lens of Agape love. This new perspective enables us to see more clearly what God's will is for us as we respond. Our response in every moment of our lives is best carried out by always being cognizant of the idea that we need God's help to achieve His perfect outcome.

Folks who realize that they can best accomplish God's will with His help will do the following:

Seek God's help frequently
Become adept at deciphering what God's will is
Be motivated to carry out God's will
Have a greater focus on God and less on themselves

How do we seek God's help? You would think this would be easy. What do we do when we need help? It depends upon the circumstances. If we have a physical emergency, we may dial 911 and ask for help. If we are having marital trouble, we may go visit a marriage counselor and ask for help. If we are having financial difficulties, we may go visit a financial advisor and ask for help. The common thread in each case when we are in need is that we "ask for help". So, given God tells us to come to Him and ask, then the act of asking should be included in every situation, every moment we live. The "ask" can be for patience, for wisdom, for provision, for healing, or for restoration of relationships among other things.

There are four passages of scripture that we should spend a moment with to address the subject "asking for God's help." The first passage appears in the book of Mark, chapter 11, verses 24-25. The passage reads, "Therefore I tell you, whatever you ask for in prayer, believe that you have received it, and it will be yours. And when you stand praying, if you hold anything against anyone, forgive him, so that your Father in heaven may forgive you your sins." There are two prerequisites to receiving a response from God to our "ask" for His help. The first is that we believe God will help us. Why would we do something if we thought our actions (in this case, prayer) would not lead to a desired outcome? Let's discuss an example. If a person wanted to lose a little weight and they saw an advertisement for a miracle weight loss pill, they may be inclined to try it if two conditions are valid. Those conditions are that the person believes the pill will achieve the desired result and that the person can afford to buy the product. Whether or not the pill will actually help the person achieve the desired result is not dependent upon whether or not the person is completely convinced the pill will work. In other words, the pill has certain properties, and those properties will either lead to weight loss or not. That fact is the same whether a person believes or does not believe the pill will help achieve weight loss. If the pill is effective, for the person to achieve the desired results they must only do one thing....swallow the pill. Likewise, the action we take to ask God to intervene in our lives or the lives of others will result in God responding if we believe He will. Applying the example to the desire to ask God for help, is it our act of prayer or our belief that God will respond to our prayer that is similar to the act of taking the pill? The answer is both. Our belief that God will answer our prayer, if we ask, is the act of taking the pill, because it is our underlying belief that the pill will help us. We can better understand Mark, chapter 11, verse 24-25 by the additional insight provided in the book of John, chapter 15, verse 7, which tells us, "If you remain in me, and my words remain in you, ask whatever you wish, and it will be given you." The word "remain" is used in this verse in the New International Version of the Bible. The English Standard Version uses the word "abide" rather than "remain". Both words are descriptive of something very important. One of the definitions of the word remain is, "to continue to possess a particular quality or fulfill a particular role." The quality to possess in the case of asking for God's help is simply acknowledging Jesus as our God. The role fulfilled is becoming a follower of Jesus. One of the definitions of the word abide is to "accept or act in accordance with a rule, decision, or recommendation." When we acknowledge Jesus as God we are motivated to act in accordance with His word. Jesus is telling us that our prayers will be answered if we are connected to Him. The reason He can say this is if we are connected to God, we will seek to do as He asks us to do. If we seek to do what He asks, we will receive the power of His love working through us. This love will guide how we pray, and more specifically, what we pray. Therefore, our prayers will be holy in terms of the fact that we will be praying God's will. That is not an easy concept to understand, let alone believe. If we pray with a pure heart (i.e. no selfish motives), God will not only hear those prayers, but intervene on our behalf because when we pray with a pure heart we are carrying out His will. God's love in us is what gives us a pure heart. The power of God's love is in us by virtue of us being willing to acknowledge He is our God and the fact that we desire to follow His words. His love in us enables our prayers to be consistent with His will.

Going back to the example, we have only discussed the scenario of the weight loss pill being effective. If the weight loss pill is not effective, then it is useless for a person to swallow the pill. If we ask God to intervene in our lives or the lives of others and we do not have full confidence that He will, it is less likely that we will realize the desired outcome. If we pray and do not have full confidence, it does not mean our prayer is useless, or God will not respond. God knows by the sheer act of praying we are demonstrating faith and sometimes our human nature is a hindrance to believing supernatural things can happen. God's love for us makes it impossible for Him to not intervene when we have love for Him, belief in who He is, and acknowledge that He can do all things.

The second prerequisite for God responding to our prayers is to avoid impeding the flow of love through ourselves by holding onto unforgiveness (refer to Mark, chapter 11, verse 25). In other words, when we ask God to intervene in our lives, if we have not forgiven someone for a wrong they did to us, our unforgiveness toward others will prevent God from forgiving us, and, hence, answering our prayers. To fully understand why God talks about unforgiveness, we need to look at additional scripture.

The next passage of scripture we need to study is found in the book of I John, chapter 4, verses 20-21. The passage reads, "If anyone says, 'I love God', yet hates his brother, he is a liar. For anyone who does not love his brother, whom he has seen, cannot love God, whom he has not seen. And He has given us this command: Whoever loves God must also love his brother." It is obvious that holding unforgiveness toward another is not loving them. God is telling us that to show we love Him, we must love our brother and sister. We must love all people. It is not possible to love God and hate others. The power of God's Agape love cannot reside within us, and flow through us, with hate in our hearts toward others. God will not be deceived. He knows our heart. He knows our every thought. If we say we love Him, but hold unforgiveness toward a brother or sister, we would be foolish to expect God to answer our prayers.

Let's examine two additional verses related to the subject of asking for God's help. The next verse is found in the book of John, chapter 3, verse 27. God tells us, "A person can receive only what is given them from heaven." The final verse to examine regarding asking for God's help is found in the book of James, chapter 1, verse 17, which reads, "Every good and perfect gift is from above, coming down from the Father of the heavenly lights, who does not change like the shifting shadows." When we ask God to help us, those requests must be holy and consistent with goodness. By communicating to us through these two verses, God is saying that what we should want to receive, and anything that is of value we receive, can only come from God. In other words, if we receive anything from another source, the gift will be less than what is best for us. That doesn't make it necessarily bad, just not optimal. To illustrate, let's assume a friend who knows you well gives you a gift that makes you happy. Although that is a very good thing, the gift that your friend gave you cannot compare with the gifts that God can give us.

The implication that the best gifts we receive only come from heaven is a clear reference to the place where God resides. Therefore, He is the source. There is no other way for us to receive help other than from God. Supernatural intervention is the only way to achieve God's best in our lives. The final verse further demonstrates that everything that comes from God is not only good for us, but perfect for us. God adds that He does not change, reinforcing the concept in our minds that we can always count on Him. If you think about it, we are talking about a being, God the Father, Jesus Christ, and the Holy Spirit, who is perfect. Why would this being ever change? If you believe God did change, you would have to admit that either the former or latter nature of God would be imperfect. However, since God is perfect, there is no need for Him to change, nor can He change, as His very nature would change to something that would differ from perfection.

Now we can move on to the second trait of folks who realize that they can best accomplish God's will with His help. They will become adept at deciphering what God's will is. Many people struggle with understanding what God's will is as we discussed earlier in this chapter. Once we understand what His overall will is, we can apply that understanding every moment of each day, in every situation we encounter, every decision we make, and every plan we contemplate. The more we do this, the better we become at ensuring that God's will becomes part of our thinking constantly. The process of improving how well we incorporate God's will into every thought and every action is called sanctification. We discussed sanctification in chapter 3 in connection with God's love. We also discussed sanctification earlier in this chapter. The understanding of the concept of sanctification deepens as we experience the flow of God's love through us, which enables us to not only defeat sin (as we read in chapter 3), thereby becoming more holy in our thinking and doing, but also enables us to fully grasp what God's will is and apply it to our lives.

Every thought we have, whether or not that thought leads to an associated action, should be assessed as a holy or unholy thought. This internal assessment is not for the purpose of self-condemnation for having an unholy thought, but for self-improvement. This self-improvement occurs as we become better at recognizing the unholy thoughts sooner and discarding them before those thoughts have a chance to influence our behavior. The power of God's Agape love overcomes the unholy thoughts we have because it is impossible to have a holy and unholy thought simultaneously.

As we experience an increasing number of holy thoughts and actions, as well as the joy associated with the corresponding increase in the amount of Agape love flowing through us, there is a natural motivation to want to experience more of this joy. That motivation is the third trait of those who realize that they can best accomplish God's will with His help. Consider for a moment something you have eaten that you absolutely love. In fact, you would call it your favorite thing to eat. Now, either think about the first time you ate your favorite food or how you feel when you eat your favorite food. Chances are thinking about your favorite food elicits an extremely nice feeling or pleasant memory. There is little doubt that you will partake in your favorite food whenever the opportunity arises because of how much you enjoy it. The same thinking occurs when we experience joy as a result of living in accordance with God's will. In fact, God tells us that the joy we experience and desire more of will strengthen us to continue to vigorously pursue more of His will in our lives. Furthermore, over time, this motivation to experience joy becomes a much more powerful force in our lives than any desire to please ourselves with something the world has to offer.

So, why don't more people demonstrate a fervor and strong pursuit of joy? There are two primary reasons. The first is a person has not experienced the joy we are talking about. That does not mean they have never loved someone, but rather the love they expressed toward another is Phileo love rather than Agape love. The second reason people do not pursue joy by carrying out God's will is that they are distracted by the cares of the world. In other words, many people are so consumed with struggling through life (i.e. paying the bills, working long hours, single parenting, trying to hold a marriage together, protecting themselves from extreme feelings of loneliness, worries about their children, or concern about whom they will marry) that those struggles become a burden. The struggles of life wear on people emotionally, draining energy, which leads to reduced effort in the area of life that is most important. This becomes a real dilemma for many because the very actions that need to be taken that will benefit us the most require energy and effort. It does take effort to love someone, but the irony is when we love someone with Agape love, it is such a joy that the effort we put into loving someone is well worth it! That joy we receive motivates us to continue to love again and again. In a true sense of the word, we become addicted to the joy and, therefore, addicted to the actions that lead to the joy.

The fourth characteristic apparent in people who realize that they can best accomplish God's will with His help is that these folks will have a greater focus on God and less on themselves. That statement should make perfect sense. If you know you need God's help to accomplish His will you must be recognizing the power of His love and the fact that you do not naturally possess it. We know we have a need and we know only He can provide what is needed. Therefore, we ask Him to help us. When we ask Him to help us we are inviting Him to speak to us and work through us to overcome our sin nature. Overcoming our sin nature enables us to be a conduit of God's Agape love. Being a conduit of God's Agape love leads to joy. It all sounds simple, right? The steps you take to accomplish God's will are not complicated. The act of taking those steps is interfered with by the cares of the world and the effect the cares of the world have on our emotions and energy. What can help us overcome the forces that are working against us? The answer is prayer. Prayer is the next aspect of God's will to be reviewed.

Many people seem to either overcomplicate prayer or misunderstand what prayer is, how to pray, and when to pray. Let's begin with a fundamental truth about prayer. Prayer is simply talking to God. If you are comfortable talking to your best friend, then you should be comfortable talking to God. When you talk to Him, He deserves reverence and respect. We need to demonstrate that to Him. The best source of instruction regarding prayer is found in the book of Matthew, chapter 6, verses 5-13. The scripture reads, "And when you pray, do not be like the hypocrites, for they love to pray standing in the synagogues and on the street corners to be seen by others. Truly I tell you, they have received their reward in full. But when you pray, go into your room, close the door and pray to your Father, who is unseen. Then your Father, who sees what is done in secret, will reward you. And when you pray, do not keep on babbling like pagans, for they think they will be heard because of their many words. Do not be like them, for your Father knows what you need before you ask him. This, then, is how you should pray: Our Father in heaven, hallowed be your name, your kingdom come, your will be done, on earth as it is in heaven. Give us today our daily bread. And forgive us our debts, as we also have forgiven our debtors. And lead us not into temptation, but deliver us from the evil one."

This passage of scripture contains much guidance. It does show us how we should have reverence for God and what we should pray for.

After acknowledging who God is, the passage immediately says to pray that "your will be done, on earth as it is in heaven."

This entire chapter has been about identifying God's will. Now we see from the passage in the book of Matthew that our prayers should include asking God to help ensure His will is done on earth. Since God is asking us to pray that His will be done, it must be His will that we pray inasmuch as asking for God to intervene is essential to accomplishing His will. In addition, we should never take the provision in our lives for granted. We acknowledge that all we have comes from God and that we humbly ask daily for food to sustain us physically. Another important item to ask God for is forgiveness since we fall short each day in living a life completely holy and pleasing to Him. That forgiveness will be given, but only if we forgive others who have wronged us in some way. Lastly, a vital part of our prayers should include asking for constant guidance and direction to show us how to avoid evil and to be protected from the evil temptations that we encounter each day.

The next aspect of God's will that we are going to think about is His desire for His children to spend time together. God tells us in the book of Matthew that where two or more of His children are gathered, He is there. God also tells us that He inhabits the praises of His children in the book of Psalms. Both references refer to His children getting together, although when we praise God corporately we are also praising Him individually. The most explicit verse on this subject is found in the book of Hebrews, chapter 10, verses 24-25. In this scripture God says, "And let us consider how we may spur one another on toward love and good deeds, not giving up meeting together, as some are in the habit of doing, but encouraging one another—and all the more as you see the Day approaching." The message is very clear. We are to have fellowship with each other often for some very good reasons. We are to be an example for each other by our actions and our words. When we are with other believers who are actively pursuing holiness and carrying out God's will, it is motivating. The joy that was referred to earlier is contagious. Being reminded of where that joy comes from is extremely motivating. The act of sharing our experiences of loving others and the good deeds associated with loving others is in itself giving Agape love.

Another good reason for fellowshipping with other believers is to encourage. During our time on earth we will experience sickness, be subjected to hate or unfair representations of who we are, be ridiculed for our faith, and, in extreme cases, physically harassed. When any of these negative experiences happen, it is very healthy to be around other believers to receive encouragement.

God identifies the benefit of being with other believers in the book of Proverbs, chapter 27, verse 17 when He states, "As iron sharpens iron, so one person sharpens another." If you have two iron blades that are used repeatedly but never sharpened against each other, the blades will tend to become dull over time and less effective for the intended purpose. Alternatively, if the iron blades are rubbed against each other periodically the blades will retain a sharpened edge that enhances the ability of the blade to carry out its' intended purpose. In the same way, when believers come together, there is a spiritual sharpening that takes place. This sharpening process can only be good and will certainly lead to each person's life being more effective in fulfilling God's will.

One other important reason to fellowship with other believers is for the transfer of wisdom and knowledge. God tells us in the book of Romans, chapter 15, verse 14, that "I myself am convinced, my brothers and sisters, that you yourselves are full of goodness, filled with knowledge and competent to instruct one another." As we gain wisdom and knowledge by understanding more of the truth, it is incumbent upon us to not only use this wisdom and knowledge in our own lives, but pass this wisdom and knowledge along for the benefit of others.

Taking the previous thought a step further leads us to another important part of God's will. He not only wants us to share His wisdom and knowledge with other believers, but He wants us to share His truths and wisdom and knowledge with unbelievers. In the book of Matthew, chapter 28, verses 19-20, God commands us to, "Therefore go and make disciples of all nations, baptizing them in the name of the Father and of the Son and of the Holy Spirit, and teaching them to obey everything I have commanded you." The instruction here is that for those who know the truth to share it with others. Once a person understands and acknowledges the truth, we are to baptize and teach them.

When we do what God has asked us, we are doing His will. Not everything that happens is God's will. This is contrary to what some people think. You have probably heard someone say, "Well, I guess it was God's will" after something bad happened to them. That is an inaccurate use of the term God's will. God loves us and does not orchestrate bad things that happen. The bad things (including physical death) happen because we live in a fallen, sinful world and sometimes because of the decisions we make. God does promise to take the bad things that happen to us and turn them into something good. It is hard for many people to accept the last statement. Only two conditions need to be met to realize the good that can come from every bad or evil act. The first is we must trust that God will intervene and some good will occur. The second is that we must change our focus as we move forward beyond the bad thing that has happened. This change in focus comes with a better understanding of God's will. As a person understands and focuses more on God's will, there is a paradigm shift in the person's mind when looking at every situation in life. For example, when someone we love dies, we will grieve over the loss regardless of whether or not we understand God's will. A person with an understanding of God's will realizes that God's will is for the deceased person to be with Him forever, not to orchestrate events that lead to the person's passing. Let me give you a specific example from my life. I was married to a woman named Brenda and had four beautiful children with her. Brenda and I loved our children and the privilege of raising them. Brenda prematurely made her way to heaven at the age of 50 due to complications from a battle with breast cancer. I could not explain to our children why Brenda would leave earth so soon but I told them to focus on where she is now and how she now lacks sickness and pain. In fact, the sickness and pain has been replaced with immense joy and peace. Less than two and one-half years after Brenda's passing, God answered my prayers to heal my emotions and the pain of loneliness. God put Melissa in my life. We were married and God blessed us with three beautiful children. The fact that something bad happened was turned into good. God had nothing to do with the bad and everything to do with the good. The hardest part for many of us is trusting that God will turn what was meant for evil into good. That trust is always put to the test during times of great trials in our lives, so we need a strong faith and patience. It is not easy and, in my case, I will gladly admit there were some very difficult days between Brenda's passing and the day Melissa and I were married. Days filled with enormous discouragement and sadness. I could only rely on faith that God would intervene and trust that what He said would happen. That focus, along with the belief that Brenda was experiencing complete joy, enabled me to continue to function and try to fulfill the role God gave me as father to my children. As difficult as certain trials can be for any of us, we must never lose hope and always keep doing what God has asked us to do.

The last aspect of God's will that will be presented in this book is God's desire for us to understand Him more. How do we know this? Throughout the Bible, God gives us information about Himself. One example is when He tells us in the book of 2 Peter, chapter 3, verse 8,

"But do not forget this one thing, dear friends: With the Lord a day is like a thousand years, and a thousand years are like a day. The Lord is not slow in keeping his promise, as some understand slowness." This verse is intended to show us that we serve a God who loves us so much that He is willing to wait for us to repent. It also gives us insight into God's existence relative to time. Scripture is full of revelation about who God is. He intended to reveal these things to us because He wants us to understand Him....at least as much as our finite minds can comprehend. Before sharing more scripture about understanding God, it is important to take the scripture just quoted in 2 Peter a bit deeper. The first sentence of this passage is, for many, difficult to understand. Essentially, God exists outside the realm of time. So, what does that mean? The specific wording in the scripture gives us the answer. If a day is like a thousand years and a thousand years are like a day, time is irrelevant to God. That does not mean time is meaningless, just that God transcends the boundaries of time. He operates beyond the constraints of time. He always was, and always will be. Therefore, He is infinite. When Jesus came to earth, He was forced to live within the constraints of time. In fact, He made statements such as "it is not time" or "the day will come" or "in time I will return". Hence, He recognized that a certain amount of time must pass before something occurred. Jesus is obviously cognizant of time, but He exists outside of time when He was not on the earth. Therefore, you can conclude that His patience toward us is only limited to the time we spend on earth. If a person has not repented by the time they take their last breath on earth, it is clear that they will not partake in the kingdom of God. That outcome, however, is not God's will.

There are numerous examples proving God's desire for us to gain understanding about Him and His truths. In the book of Proverbs, chapter 2, verses 1-5, God says, "My son, if you accept my words and store up my commands within you, turning your ear to wisdom and applying your heart to understanding, and if you call out for insight and cry aloud for understanding, and if you look for it as for silver and search for it as for hidden treasure, then you will understand the fear of the Lord and find the knowledge of God." To obtain some of God's knowledge is to gain insight into who He is. God is obviously encouraging us to do just that.

Every scripture is intended to teach us who God is, and what He expects of us. His will is for us to know Him better, to love Him as He loves us, and to serve Him by carrying out His will during our time on earth. When you consider why He made us, you should be convinced that He wants to have a relationship with you. When you have a relationship with someone, to become close you must get to know each other deeply. The same applies to our relationship with God. The only difference is He already knows everything about us while we come into existence having to spend our entire lives learning about Him. And, that is exactly what He wants. The elementary knowledge about God that He shares with us is not difficult to understand, but as you dig deeper you will find the concepts about God and what He expects become more difficult for our finite minds to process. That is one reason He tells us to be still, to meditate upon His word, and to seek to understand more about Him daily. The benefits of doing these things have been discussed in prior chapters of this book so there is no need to reiterate now. However, suffice it to say that our ultimate reward (eternal life) makes the effort to gain understanding and knowledge of God and His truths well worth it. We will spend the next chapter discussing more thoroughly our ultimate reward as well as the earthly blessings that come from serving God, pursuing Him, and carrying out His will.

CHAPTER 9

Heavenly Blessings vs. Earthly Blessings

As we delve into the subject matter regarding blessings, we must define what a blessing is and how these blessings originate. In Webster's dictionary, one of the definitions of the word blessing reads, "Any means of happiness; a gift, benefit or advantage; that which promotes temporal prosperity and welfare, or secures immortal felicity." The word felicity means great happiness and the joys of heaven. That definition may not help you fully know the difference between heavenly blessings and earthly blessings. But, at least you know both kinds of blessings have to be good and involve creating joy and happiness. The blessings we receive can be considered gifts. We are not the source of those gifts when we are the recipient of a gift/blessing. Conversely, we can be the source of a blessing for another recipient. Whomever is the source is actually an intermediary source as the true source of a blessing (whether we are giving a blessing or receiving a blessing) is always God. Some blessings occur without an intermediary. For example, when God designed our physical bodies, He designed them with an immune system to fight disease; with the ability to heal wounds, and with the ability to filter toxins out of our blood to be removed from our bodies. This design created by God is a blessing. Going back to the definition of a blessing, the fact that our bodies have been designed to fight disease and heal certainly contributes to temporal welfare, and, in this case, the temporal welfare is physical welfare. Someone may argue that not all bodies work the way I described. If some have a compromised immune system or a disease that slows or interferes with the healing process, that does not negate in any way the truth about God's design. What it does mean is that some people's bodies do not work as intended. That is typically no fault of their own.

A second example of a blessing directly from God without an intermediary is the gift of grace which leads to salvation. Again, remember a blessing is a gift. The gift of grace, if accepted, secures immortal felicity, or eternal life in heaven. Receiving this gift gives a person much happiness knowing eternal joy has become a reality. Furthermore, when our physical body dies, the reality of eternal joy begins. This is the best example of a blessing that provides immediate benefit and future benefit.

Whether the blessing is through an intermediary or directly from God, all blessings can be categorized as either heavenly blessings or earthly blessings. The categorization does not refer to the source of the blessing, as all blessings come from God, and He is everywhere. The categorization does refer to where the recipient experiences the blessing. The example of how our physical bodies have been designed with an immune system is an earthly blessing. The example of the blessing of eternal life is a heavenly blessing. Let's review a few more examples to illustrate the point and further differentiate earthly from heavenly blessings.

If a person drives a vehicle that become inoperable, and has a strong need for transportation, meeting that need becomes a blessing. The person who is in need of reliable transportation becomes the recipient of the blessing when the need is met. Let's assume that a friend of the person who needs reliable transportation becomes aware of the need and volunteers to pick up the person and take them to work. The friend is the intermediary source of the blessing and the person who received a ride to work is the recipient of the blessing. The ultimate source of the blessing is God inasmuch as the act of providing a ride is an act of serving and loving another person. The intermediary source was motivated by love (God) to help their friend. The blessing in this case is an earthly blessing.

A second example involves a couple who desire to have a child. They have been married for seven years and have taken no precautions to prevent a pregnancy. After exhausting all efforts known to the medical profession, it has been determined that, short of a miracle, the couple will not be able to conceive. Doctors have been wrong and miracles can happen, however, doctors are correct much more often than not and, although miracles occur every day, miracles do not occur every day in every situation that we would want to be changed miraculously. For the example of the childless couple, we will assume that a biological miracle for the couple is not likely. The couple, however, do not lose hope. They know God has told them that He will grant them the desires of their heart. One specific instance in scripture is found in the book of Psalms, chapter 37, verses 3-4, which reads, "Trust in the Lord and do good; dwell in the land and enjoy safe pasture. Delight yourself in the Lord and He will give you the desires of your heart." God is telling us that if we pursue holiness and are obedient to Him, our lives will be better in many ways. We will never lack provision in our lives to meet our needs. Our prayers will be guided by holy desires. In the example of the childless couple, their prayers for a child certainly qualify as a holy desire. Unselfish acts, as we discussed earlier in this book, are holy acts because our focus is on God and others rather than ourselves. After much prayer about their desire to be parents, the couple in our example decide to attempt to adopt. They contacted an adoption agency and began the process. This particular adoption agency asks the couple to prepare a portfolio of pictures of their home and life together, as well as a narrative regarding the story of their lives and why they want to be parents. As young girls or young women find themselves in a difficult crisis pregnancy situation, they are referred to this adoption agency. At the adoption agency, the pregnant girls/women review the portfolios of various couples, ultimately selecting the couple they are most comfortable with raising the child they are carrying. One day not long after the completion of the preparation of the portfolio, the childless couple receive a phone call from the adoption agency informing them that a birthmother has selected them to raise the unborn child. You can imagine the excitement the couple experienced when they heard the news. A few months later the child was born and the couple experienced joy (the flow of love) as they held their newborn child for the first time. This is an example of an earthly blessing, because of where the couple received the blessing.

In chapter 8 we discussed the impact of experiencing joy vs. being burdened by the cares of the world. When you receive a blessing, the blessing extinguishes completely the cares of the world during the moments you are experiencing the blessing. One reason why the burdens of living on earth are lifted completely at the moment we recognize that we have received a blessing is that the emotion of joy supersedes all other emotions. Earlier in the book we discussed the death of a loved one. Obviously, there is an intense sadness associated with the loss. That sadness can be temporarily lifted by a blessing. The only way that is possible is the joy associated with the blessing received is a stronger emotion than the sadness we feel associated with the passing of a loved one.

Blessings can be answers to prayer or someone motivated by love, or both. For the former, the childless couple prayed for a child and God intervened as only He can. For the latter, the friend who provided a ride for the person without transportation is an example of a blessing that was given by someone motivated by love. Now, you could say that when God intervenes He is motivated by love....and you would be right! The most important learning about blessings is that love is involved every time. To prove this, I would challenge you to think of a blessing in your life. Once you have thought of a particular blessing, consider whether or not love was involved. Most people would agree that having daily provision of food is a blessing. How is love involved in that blessing? God tells us that He provides all things including our daily bread. In fact, we are to pray, and be thankful, for provision every day. God is clearly motivated by love when He provides for us.

The truth that blessings are motivated by love can be used to not only determine what a blessing is, but also point out that, sometimes, what we label as blessings are not. For example, one Sunday afternoon you go to a restaurant, have a meal, and are presented with your bill. After reviewing your bill, it is apparent that the server neglected to charge you for one of the items you ordered. If the omission of the item on your bill was a mistake made by your server, the omission was not motivated by love. Therefore, in this case, not being charged for something you received is not a blessing. However, if the server or manager of the restaurant felt as though you should not be charged for an item because it was delivered late or the quality was not their typical standard, the answer is different. The server or manager in the latter case wants you to know they felt bad about the situation and wanted to do something for you to show you they care about you. They, of course, want you to return to the restaurant. In this case not being charged for the item would be a blessing because the server and/or manager were motivated by love, whether or not they realized it. Anytime you show concern for someone, love is involved. Let's consider two more cases of the restaurant example. The next case is that you received your food item and it was not edible because it was either not cooked enough or overcooked. You then told the server, who takes the food back and has it prepared correctly. The server did what he/she had to do but did not apologize or show any indication that he/she felt bad. This is not a blessing because the action taken by the server was demanded by the customer and the server was not motivated by love. However, if, when you brought the problem to the attention of the server, he/she apologized profusely before quickly rectifying the situation with a replacement item prepared correctly, and offered you a free dessert, that would be a blessing. The condition of the heart of the person giving the blessing, not just the associated actions, is what determines whether or not what you received is a blessing. The final restaurant example is, after you finish eating, you ask the server for the bill. The server informs you that another restaurant patron paid your bill. The person who paid for your meal has never met you, and, in fact, left the restaurant before you were informed your bill was paid. This is a blessing inasmuch as the restaurant customer who paid your bill was motivated by love, Agape love. The customer does not know you but wanted to bless you.

To reiterate a point made earlier, there is always joy in receiving a blessing and in giving a blessing. The joy experienced by the receiver will eventually motivate them to give a blessing to others. The reason I say eventually is that the action to give a blessing by the one who received a blessing is partly dependent upon the condition of the person's heart. In other words, if the person who received the blessing is not connected to God and, prior to receiving the blessing, had not often or ever experienced the joy that comes from Agape love, a process of softening of the heart needs to occur. It is impossible to predict how long this process will take, but you can be assured the process will take place if a person is surrounded by Agape love received from God directly or God working through others to deliver Agape love to the person. As we discussed earlier in this book, receiving Agape love will make people think about the reality of God and draw them closer to having a relationship with Him.

The joy experienced by the giver motivates them to continue to give additional blessings. This joy is a strengthening of the soul and an excitement because of the ability to witness God's Agape love in action. Furthermore, there is a humble gratefulness tied to the realization that, as a giver, are privileged and able to be part of God's work on earth. If you ask anyone who lives each day being a conduit of God's love how the experience of giving a blessing feels, you will undoubtedly hear sentiment such as "there is no greater feeling", or "nothing can surpass the joy of giving", or "until I started truly giving blessings to others, I did not know what I was missing", or "the joy I experience in giving blessings makes me want more of the same feeling." Many of you reading this book have experienced the joy that comes from giving a blessing. For you, there is no need to explain what it feels like. If you have any doubt whether you have or have not experienced the joy we are talking about, just look for the next opportunity to give a blessing and you will no longer have doubt.

The remainder of this chapter will be devoted to a discussion of a few blessings that are less tangible, but extremely valuable in terms of building deep relationships with others. God has much to say about being honest. Even secular psychologists and those who study interpersonal interactions from a non-Biblical world view purport that the most rewarding, deepest, and long-lasting healthy relationships are those built upon trust. We also know that one of the best ways to build trust with another person is to be completely honest with them. It is indeed refreshing to have dialogue with another person who has nothing to hide, is not pretending to be someone they are not, and desires a complete, open, and honest exchange of thoughts and ideas. God, who made us and knows us better than anyone, has issued warnings to not lie, and He also speaks of the blessing given and received in honest interactions. He says in the book of Deuteronomy, chapter 5, verse 20 that, "You shall not give false testimony against your neighbor." He tells us in the book of Proverbs, chapter 6, verses 16-19 that, "There are six things the Lord hates, seven that are detestable to Him: haughty eyes, a lying tongue, hands that shed innocent blood, a heart that devises wicked schemes, feet that are quick to rush into evil, a false witness who pours out lies, and a man who stirs up dissension among brothers." Lying is mentioned twice among the seven things God finds detestable.

He knows the damage lying can do to the relationship between people and how, for the one who lies, lying weakens the pursuit of holiness and the ability to do what is good in the eyes of God. In the book of John, chapter 8, verse 44, Jesus is quoted directly as He responds to the Pharisees, "You belong to your father, the devil, and you want to carry out your father's desire. He was a murderer from the beginning, not holding to the truth, for there is no truth in him. When he lies, he speaks his native language, for he is a liar and the father of lies." When a person lies, they are in the company of the devil. That is probably not something any of us would ever want!

There are also many scriptures regarding honesty. Just a few will be cited here. In the book of Proverbs, chapter 16, verse 13, God says, "Kings take pleasure in honest lips; they value a man who speaks the truth." The use of the term King is intentional and holds a deeper meaning. One of the functions of the King was to serve as judge. The King had to decipher between truth and untruth before passing judgement. To carry out the role of judge, the King's job was made much easier by those who spoke the truth. In the book of Proverbs, chapter 24, verse 26, God tells us that, "An honest answer is like a kiss on the lips." This is directly correlated with a blessing. The person being honest with us is giving us a blessing. It not only makes the giver and receiver experience joy, but the relationship between the two people grows deeper. In the book of 1

Corinthians, chapter 13, verse 6, God tells us, "Love does not delight in evil but rejoices with the truth." The love referred to in this verse is Agape love. Whether you are the giver or receiver, you enjoy honesty because the communication is driven by love rather than hate. For those of you who have children, you can think of examples in your own life through your interaction with your children that make you rejoice in the truth. If your child has done something they should not do, and they come to you and tell the truth about what they did, you may not be happy about what they did that they should not have done, but you are pleased that they told you the truth. A parent is filled with love and receives joy when a child is able to overcome the temptation to lie, particularly when they believe there will be consequences as a result of their disobedience. The same is true for adults. Most people value the truth from another person more than just focusing on what the other person did or did not do. A quick example may help illustrate the point. Let's assume a husband is at work and his wife calls him and asks him to pick up a couple of things at the grocery store on his way home and he forgets. He arrives home and his wife asks if he stopped at the grocery store on the way home to pick up what she asked. If the husband makes up a lie such as that he did stop but the store had none of the items she asked for, that harms their relationship and makes both of them miss out on joy. If the husband expresses sorrow and apologizes for forgetting to stop at the grocery store and offers to go back out to the store, the message to his wife is one of love. He demonstrates that he is sorry for letting her down and offers to make up for his mistake. She would much rather hear the truth and be willing to forgive her husband for forgetting to stop at the store on the way home than to hear a lie and feel disrespected and unloved. Appropriately, the next blessing to be examined is forgiveness.

The concept of forgiveness is mentioned 96 times in the NIV version of the Bible. Sounds like God wants to highlight the importance of us forgiving another person. There is more to forgiveness than most of us realize. When someone hurts you in some way, there is no guarantee that the person who hurt you will ask you to forgive them. If they do not ask for forgiveness, does that mean we do not have to forgive them? Of course not. Jesus forgave those who crucified Him without them asking for forgiveness. The specific scripture is found the book of Luke, chapter 23, verses 33-34, which reads, "When they came to the place called the Skull, there they crucified Him, along with the criminals; one on His right, the other on His left. Jesus said, Father, forgive them, for they do not know what they are doing." Another equally extreme example of forgiveness is when Stephen was being stoned by the Sanhedrin. In the book of Acts, chapter 7, verses 59-60, God tell us, "While they were stoning him, Stephen prayed, 'Lord Jesus, receive my spirit'. Then he fell on his knees and cried out, 'Lord, do not hold this sin against them'. When he had said this, he fell asleep." Falling asleep referred to dying. These examples of forgiveness are, hopefully, experiences we will not have to encounter. However, even without the experience of being persecuted unto death, we will have many other types of hurts that come our way initiated by others. Some people will gossip about us. Some people will lie to us. Some people will steal from us. Some people will ridicule us because they do not agree with what we believe. These are a few categories of the types of ways that people may hurt us. Most people can think of examples from each of these categories regarding how someone hurt them. The hurt experienced lingers when one condition exists. The condition is a particular state of mind. The condition is unforgiveness. If we do not forgive the person who hurt us, we remind ourselves repeatedly of the wrong that was done to us. When we dwell on the wrong done to us, we fan the flames of unforgiveness, and the accompanying anger, bitterness, resentment, and, in many cases, hatred toward the person who hurt us. If we experience these feelings toward the person who hurts us, we are obviously not loving the person who hurt us. These feelings will prevent us from loving others with Agape love as God has asked us. In the book of Ephesians, chapter 4, verses

26-27 God tells us, "In your anger do not sin: Do not let the sun go down while you are still angry, and do not give the devil a foothold." Well, you now know the timing regarding holding on to anger toward another. God makes it clear that we should get rid of our anger before the day is over. As you know, some people remain angry for days, weeks, months, or even years. During the time people are angry, they are not loving others. When they are not loving they are not living in accordance to God's command. When they are not living in accordance to God's command they are more susceptible to sin. Whether a person knows it or not, embracing and holding on to anger, bitterness, resentment, etc. prevents a person from becoming all that God wants them to be. Most importantly, the conduit of Agape love that God asks us to be is impossible to achieve while we are harboring unforgiveness toward another person. And, as we learned in a prior chapter of this book, without the flow of Agape love through us we cannot experience true joy.

Given the serious ramifications of unforgiveness, how do we avoid living with unforgiveness in our soul? Well, God tells us in the same chapter of Ephesians, verse 29 to, "not let any unwholesome talk come out of your mouths, but only what is helpful for building others up according to their needs, that it may benefit those who listen." In this passage, God highlights what we say since our anger can quickly manifest itself in hurtful words toward another person. Worldly advice from behavioral psychologists and others tell us that when feelings of anger arise, take a deep breath and count to ten before responding to the stimuli, or circumstances that led to our feelings of anger. That is not ineffective advice, however, there is a course of action that is much more effective. God continues in verses 31-32 of the same chapter of Ephesians by telling us to, "Get rid of all bitterness, rage and anger, brawling and slander, along with every form of malice. Be kind and compassionate to one another, forgiving each other, just as Christ God forgave you."

God never gives us a command that is unachievable. He does give us commands that require us to put forth effort. He also gives us the ability to do what He asks. The answer to how we can be compassionate and forgiving rather than angry and bitter is found in the next passage in Ephesians, which is chapter 5, verses 1-2. God says, "Be imitators of God, therefore, as dearly loved children and live a life of love, just as Christ loved us and gave Himself up for us as a fragrant offering and sacrifice to God." The answer is to live a life of love. We can only do that with God's help, as discussed earlier in this book. When we develop a habit of living a life of love, we reap the benefits of the gifts of the Holy Spirit, which include love, joy peace, patience, and kindness.

Just to reiterate, please know that there is nothing stronger than the power of Agape love. The flow of Agape love enables us to be compassionate and forgiving when people hurt us. It also enables us to be compassionate and forgiving when people do not hurt us. Agape love infused into every thought we have and action we take leads to maximizing the effect of that love on our own being, which brings supernatural joy and strength to our soul, and touches every other person we come in contact with during our time on earth. When you forgive someone, you are infused with Agape love. When you are infused with Agape love, it is easy to forgive. This may sound like double speak to you, or a chicken or the egg dilemma. However, these two thoughts are both independent and interdependent.

The reason these thoughts are interdependent is that the act of forgiveness is expressing love toward another person. In other words, when we forgive, Agape love is at work within us. We become better at forgiving the more we experience giving Agape love. We also become better at giving Agape love the more we forgive.

Now, let's see how the independency of giving Agape love and forgiving is different than the interdependency of these two behaviors. When we are born into this world, we possess a sin nature. Our natural sinful state is void of Agape love. We may experience Agape love many times before we forgive. When we encounter Agape love as a recipient, we are not forgiving anyone, but rather receiving. That is evidence that the experience of Agape love is independent of the act of forgiving another person. The more we give and receive Agape love, the more Agape love becomes infused in our thoughts and our actions.

To summarize, interdependency exists since you, as a giver or receiver, cannot experience forgiveness without experiencing Agape love. Separately, we have cited many examples of how you can receive Agape love without forgiving someone. That means the giving and receiving of Agape love and forgiving someone or being forgiven can be experiences that are independent.

Do not underestimate the power of forgiveness. Relationships between any two or more people are strengthened on the back of forgiveness. Forgiveness doesn't have to be given only in the event of a major hurt. There are often acts of rudeness that seem very minor, but still require forgiveness. For example, if you are driving in a long line of traffic and another driver bypasses the line of traffic by driving on the shoulder of the road to save themselves time, you may believe that is rude and inconsiderate behavior. You may be correct. If so, you may let the other person's behavior get under your skin and become irritated or even angry. God tells us to forgive for our own benefit as well. The other driver may never know the actions he/she took caused you to have feelings of anger. In addition, the other driver may never know you also immediately forgave him/her for being inconsiderate (if that is what you did), but the ramifications of forgiveness not given would prevent you from being a conduit of God's love and make you susceptible to other kinds of sin. In addition, let's further assume there was one other important fact you did not know about the other driver's behavior. That fact is the other driver had a passenger who was experiencing a medical emergency and every moment was vital to the well-being of the passenger. If you knew that fact, wouldn't that knowledge tend to diffuse your initial feelings of irritation or anger toward the other driver? Furthermore, wouldn't you do the same thing as the other driver if you were trying to get your passenger to a medical facility as fast as possible given the medical emergency? Making assumptions without all the facts can lead to feelings based upon inaccurate assessments of circumstances. The best way to avoid making inaccurate assessments of circumstances is to obtain as many facts as you can before concluding what you believe happened. There is one gift you can use that will empower you to collect as many facts as possible before passing judgement. That gift is patience. At the moment you are loving someone with Agape love, you will be exercising patience toward that person. Patience will enable you to take some time to collect facts before prematurely jumping to an incorrect conclusion. Let's look at one more example. Your teenage child, Matthew, is attending a school event and the curfew you have given him is 10 p.m. Matthew arrives home at 11 p.m. As a parent, you might become irritated and speak a bit harshly, saying, "I'm sorry Matthew, but you were not home by 10 p.m. so you are going to be grounded for 2 weeks." Or, in a more loving tone, you could say, "Matthew, what happened tonight that kept you out past your curfew?" Giving Matthew the opportunity to tell you why he did not arrive home until 11 p.m. is being patient with him and showing concern for him. If Matthew tells you that he does not have a good reason for arriving home late, you could, in love, still administer the disciplinary action. If, however, Matthew tells you that on his way home he helped a woman by changing a flat tire on her vehicle. You then notice his hands and clothes are dirty. He also shares with you a couple of photos he took of the flat tire and the new tire on the vehicle. Based upon the additional facts learned, you are likely to show him you appreciate what he did to help the woman and reward him for the good behavior he demonstrated. That is a very different outcome compared to what could have transpired if, the moment your son walked in the front door, you yelled at him for being late and immediately grounded him. Making assumptions is something that happens to many people every day. Some of these assumptions involve subtle experiences, but are none the less real and could influence our feelings toward the person we are making assumptions about. The effect on our demeanor toward others, the attitude we have, and the communication toward others is largely contingent upon whether or not we gather enough relevant facts to understand a situation. Gathering enough relevant facts and interpreting those facts accurately is only possible with patience. The bottom line here is patience is a blessing we can give to others. The person with whom you are patient is not only glad you were patient, but has no choice but to feel the power of God's Agape love because you were patient.

This will sound strange but patience is a blessing we can also give to ourselves. This thought is two-fold. Most people will think that when we are patient with ourselves, we are doing much self-reflection and determining what we did, and thinking about how what we did worked well or did not work well. Through this self-examination, if we do not beat ourselves up for handling a situation in a less than optimal manner, we are being patient with ourselves. If we are encouraged by how we handled a situation, we should take the time to recognize that our behavior was good. This type of patience with ourselves is beneficial to reinforce the positive behavior or identify ways we can improve a negative behavior. The importance of self-reflection cannot be overstated. The second way we receive a blessing when we are patient is not related to being patient with our own behavior, but rather the blessing we receive when we are patient with others. This should make sense given what we learned earlier in this book. When we are patient with others, we are loving them. When we are loving them, we are experiencing joy. Joy is the blessing!

The final blessing to be discussed is compassion. We can only be compassionate to others if motivated by Agape love. God commands us to have compassion for others. In the book of 1 Peter, chapter 3, verse 8 God tells us, "Finally, all of you, be like-minded, be sympathetic, love one another, be compassionate and humble." God is telling us we should all be doing the same thing with regard to having compassion for each other, and, He is telling us that being compassionate is loving each other. Conversely, you should conclude if you are not compassionate with another person, you are not loving them. A corroborating verse is found in the book of Colossians, chapter 3, verse 12, which reads, "Therefore, as God's chosen people, holy and dearly loved, clothe yourselves with compassion, kindness, humility, gentleness and patience." Our demeanor, temperament, and behavior should be all of these things. However, remember these attributes are not natural for us, but can be ours everyday with the flow of Agape love through us. God tells us in the book of Romans, chapter 12, verse 15 to, "Rejoice with those who rejoice; mourn with those who mourn." When someone shares news with you, the feelings they are experiencing should be mimicked within us. We should ask ourselves if we really feel happy for someone when they share good news about themselves with us. Likewise, when someone shares bad news about themselves, do we really understand and feel the sadness that accompanies the bad news. If we can answer yes to either of those questions, we are loving that person and showing great compassion. Next time you are in a conversation with someone, pay attention to how you feel when they share exceptionally good or bad news. Doing this will help you understand how well you are being compassionate. Do not judge yourself if your compassion output is low nor think you have it all together if your compassion output is high. If your compassion output is low, you have just identified an area of self-improvement. If your compassion output is high, you will already be experiencing the joy that loving someone brings, but keep pursuing holiness to maintain the flow of love through you. Our level of compassion is not dictated upon who we have compassion for, but rather based upon from whom gives us the ability to have compassion. God gives us the ability to have compassion for all people. Short of a powerful flow of God's love in us, we can only have compassion for those we have previously loved.

How can we put compassion into action other than to have empathy for someone or rejoicing with someone? There are clear answers in the Bible. In chapter 8 of this book we discussed God's will. Part of His will is for us to help those in need. There were several verses quoted, but one of them, found in the book of Zechariah, chapter 7, verses 9-10, gives us the connection between helping those in need and showing true compassion. The verses read, "This is what the Lord Almighty said: Administer true justice; show mercy and compassion to one another. Do not oppress the widow or the fatherless, the foreigner or the poor. Do not plot evil against each other." Helping those in need is showing compassion because we realize some people have much less than we do and we are in a position to help them meet their basic needs. Having compassion without action is better than not having compassion, however, having compassion with action activates an additional blessing that the person in need receives.

As this chapter comes to a close, there is one simple and succinct way to summarize how a person gives or receives a blessing. Giving and receiving Agape love is the source of all blessings. We mentioned a few of the most significant acts of Agape love in this chapter, which include honesty, forgiveness, patience, and compassion. There is one significant act of Agape love that is conspicuously missing from this list. That act is sacrifice. The reason we did not examine the role of sacrificing as it relates to a blessing is because sacrifice is the only way we are reconciled with God, which is the subject of the next chapter.

CHAPTER 10

Reconciliation with God

The spiritual truths discussed through the first nine chapters of this book are the keys to unlocking the doors to understanding who God is, what He expects of us, and the benefits given for us to experience during our time on earth if we focus on living our lives being conduits of His love. We have also touched upon eternal benefits that can be ours if we obey God's commands, listen to His teaching, and do His will each day. The reason a distinction is drawn between our time on earth and eternal life is to help you focus on both. We will explore more about the eternal benefits in chapter 11 as the entire chapter is focused on life after physical death. Before we delve into the subject of eternal life, it is important to understand that there is an essential action each of us must take to not only be rewarded with eternal life but also experience, during our life on earth, the full benefits God offers to us. The action we must take is in response to something God has already done for us.

In fact, what He did opens the door for us to reconcile with Him......if we respond to His offer.

In chapter two of this book we focused on spiritual forces. When we sin, we are succumbing to the force of evil. When this happens, we are being hostile to God, who is holy. We are born with a natural inclination to sin and, without God's help, we are doomed to live an unholy life. However, we should all be thanking God every day because He has intervened on our behalf. How has He intervened? Let's look a few verses of scripture. In the book of Romans, chapter 5, verses 10-11, God tells us, "For if, when we were God's enemies, we were reconciled to Him through the death of His Son, how much more, having been reconciled, shall we be saved through His life. Not only is this so, but we also rejoice in God through our Lord Jesus Christ, through whom we have now received reconciliation." We have assurance that because of what Jesus Christ did for us by sacrificing Himself on the cross, we are given the opportunity to no longer be an enemy of God. Please remember that when we live life in a sinful manner, we are doing the opposite of what God wants and, hence, are considered His enemy. Therefore, we can be certain of two things. First, if we do not repent, or turn from our sin, we miss the joy that can be experienced while on earth as well as the eternal rewards after our physical lungs take their last breath and our heart beats for the last time. Second, if we do repent and turn from our sin, God will forgive us, and help us defeat sin in our life each day. He has enabled forgiveness of sin through the sacrifice Jesus Christ made for us. He has given us His Holy Spirit to guide us, strengthen us, and empower us to defeat sin while being a conduit of Agape love. If we choose to accept what He did for us, we are taking Him up on His offer of reconciliation.

An example may help drive home the point here. I have known many people who have had a disagreement with a friend or family member.

Sometimes those disagreements led the two people who disagreed to stop talking to each other for a period of time. The period of time may be days, weeks, months, or even years. During the time the two people who disagreed had not spoken to each other, their relationship suffered deep wounds. The longer the communication standoff, the deeper the wounds. There are people who never speak to each other again. That is very sad. Most folks, however, do speak again at some point. What leads them to reconcile? One of the parties takes the initiative to contact the other and either apologize or ask for forgiveness or lets the person know how much they truly care about them; or all of the above! The relationship can be restored through the reconciliation process initiated by the person who apologizes or asks for forgiveness or let the person know how much they care about them. The person who takes the initiative is risking rejection, but that risk is always worth taking.

There is a subtle, but very important, difference in the reconciliation between ourselves and God compared to the reconciliation process between ourselves and another person we know. God is waiting for us to take the initiative to apologize and ask for forgiveness. In the case of reconciling with God, we have no risk in taking the initiative to reconcile. In other words, He loves us unconditionally and will never reject us. Furthermore, He has already done His part. He demonstrated how much He loves us dying a brutal death by crucifixion. In addition, He has told us that He will forgive us. All we need to do is repent. So, unlike the example of two humans in a disagreement, we do not have to guess how God feels about our sin or disobedience, we just have to reconcile with Him by our belief in who He is, what He has done for us, and ask for forgiveness. There is a second passage of scripture that applies here and is very similar conceptually to the scripture in chapter 5 of the book of Romans. The second passage is found in the book of Colossians, chapter 1, verses 19-22, which reads, "For God was pleased to have all His fullness dwell in Him, and through Him to reconcile to Himself all things, whether things on earth or things in heaven, by making peace through His blood, shed on the cross. Once you were alienated from God and were enemies in your minds because of your evil behavior. But now He has reconciled you by Christ's physical body through death to present you holy in His sight, without blemish and free from accusation." The message of the sacrifice God made is the same in the passage in Romans, chapter 5 and Colossians, chapter 1. God also reiterates the fact that, as sinners, we are separated from Him. He uses the term alienated, which implies there is no closeness or affection being shared. However, that lack of closeness or affection is one sided. We do not feel close to Him nor have affection for Him because of our sinful actions, however, He never stops loving us nor ceases desiring a close relationship with us. This fact, like the fact discussed previously about God always being ready to forgive us, shows how different God is from us. He is always ready to forgive, He continuously wants to be close to us. This is a different reaction from two human beings who have tension between them due to a disagreement. It is so important to see the differences between God's reaction and our reaction to similar situations. When we identify the differences, we are able to understand how we should react and how we can react with the help of His Holy Spirit working within us. In other words, we do not become God, but our actions become highly influenced by Him such that we exhibit His goodness and holiness. We can behave as He would because it is He in us that influences our behavior.

In Colossians chapter 1, notice again the use of the term "enemies". This is the same word used to describe us in Romans, chapter 5. However, this time the term is used and amplified upon with an explanation of why we are enemies. Of course, sin against God makes us His enemies, but the explanation in Colossians provides additional enlightenment. In verse 21, we deserve our designation of enemy of God because of our evil behavior. Where does this evil behavior come from? This evil behavior comes from our own actions, the genesis of which is our own minds, the prompting of which comes from Satan. God does not control our behavior. He does, however, tell us what is right to do, what is holy, and offers to help us live in a holy manner in all we do through His Holy Spirit. Ultimately, though, we have the freedom to choose holiness or sinfulness. And, as was discussed in chapter 2 of this book, there are forces at work in this spiritual tug of war.

When we reconcile with God, the best news is that the sin we committed is no longer attached to us. We are seen in God's eyes as holy and free from accusation (see verse 22). If there is no doubt someone has committed a crime, but, when they are brought before the judge, there are no accusations made, the person who committed the crime is pronounced innocent. In a court of law run by human beings, the guilty are seldom pronounced innocent, but God always proclaims our innocence because of what He did for us combined with our repentance. That is love. Since God's work is completed, all that is required for reconciliation with God is our repentance.

A third scripture succinctly emphasizes the point. In the book of Acts, chapter 3, verse 19, God tells us to, "Repent, then, and turn to God, so that your sins may be wiped out, that times of refreshing may come from the Lord." There are four key elements to this verse. The first is that we repent, or truly express both sorrow to God for what we have done and have the strong desire not to do it again. We cannot just apologize to God and continue to commit the same sin over and over again. While it is a certainty that we will sin again, the concept here is taking hold of a strong habitual pattern of sin that we actually enjoyed and turning from it. We will stumble at times, however, God will cleanse us from the sin patterns within us. This happens over time, but significant changes can occur instantaneously. God only does this within people who love Him and are motivated and willing to change their ways. This is part of the second key element of the verse; turning to God. The third key element of the verse is that God wipes our sins out. He no long holds sin against us and sin no longer separates us from God. We have covered this concept before, but it should be noted that we do not deserve what God is offering. Considering God's perfect holiness, the forgiveness He offers is something to be treasured and never taken for granted. We should not have a cavalier attitude toward what He has done for us nor should we boast or have pride because we have been forgiven. Rather, we should continually have an attitude of thankfulness and humbleness because of God's actions. The fourth key element of this verse is that times of refreshing will come from God. How good do you feel when you reconcile with a friend, family member, or spouse? No one likes the tension that can occur between people. It is at best uncomfortable and there is no complete peace within a person's soul. That is exactly why reconciliation with another person feels so good. Love is exchanged, tension dissipates, and peace returns. You feel so good you feel like celebrating. You have a bounce in your step again. You seem to have more energy. When someone asks you if you are having a good day you want to tell them how good it is! The same is true of reconciling with God. Peace returns, guilt vanishes, regret subsides, and the full flow of Agape love is activated. When the latter happens, joy is always a by-product. This is what God means by times of refreshing.

There is a type of race that has become popular in recent years called a mudder run. The race is essentially a long distance run with obstacles that make the run more difficult. The obstacles may include climbing over rock walls, running through creeks, running through muddy terrain, and crawling through pits of mud. The objective is to complete the run, not to stay clean. Participants in this type of race are guaranteed to be covered with mud from head to toe. When the participant completes the race, they are very likely to go directly to a place where they can take a shower. The shower will wash away all of the dirt on their body. The runner feels much better after the shower. We all know how it feels to be dirty and sweaty and how good a shower or bath feels. In the spiritual dimension, our soul has a similar experience when we repent of our sins and reconcile with God. There is a feeling of spiritual cleanliness, which is essentially holiness. When we repent we purge ourselves of unholy behavior, which is spiritual cleansing.

Why do some people have a difficult time reconciling with another person or with God? First, let's discuss reconciling with another person. One of the hurdles to reconciliation between people is building trust after it has been broken. Maybe you have been open and honest with someone that you thought you could trust, only to be hurt by that person. It may be difficult for you to trust the person even if they apologize for their actions. Let's assume someone hides an adulterous relationship from their spouse. At some point the truth surfaces. Even if the spouse who committed adultery seems to have a repentant heart, it may be difficult for the person who was hurt by their spouse's infidelity to trust their spouse completely. This leads us to an important question. Can you be assured that reconciliation between imperfect people is based upon honesty, truth, and transparency? The answer is that full assurance is difficult to know with certainty, however, if you are completely honest, ensure all of your statements are based upon the truth (not a distorted perspective due to personal bias), and are fully transparent, there is a very good chance the person you are reconciling with will reciprocate the same behavior. If you are expressing love toward the person you are attempting to reconcile with, it will be much easier to be completely honest, speak in truth, and be fully transparent.

Another impediment to reconciliation between people is pride. In the book of Proverbs, chapter 13, verse 10, God says, "Where there is strife, there is pride, but wisdom is found in those who take advice." Pride is the antithesis of love. Pride is selfish thinking. Love is thinking of others first. Pride convinces a person they are correct even when they are not correct. Pride is closely correlated to self-deception. Love is willing to admit fault or that you were wrong in something you said or have done. Pride is not interested in hearing how another person feels when they are trying to reconcile. Love is open to listening to another person's point of view, understanding their perspective, and using that understanding to build a bridge to reconciliation. Reflecting on Proverbs 13:10, if pride is removed, a major hurdle to reconciliation is also removed. The second part of the verse emphasizes how wise it is to listen and take advice. If we were perfect, we would not need advice. However, our imperfections always give rise to opportunities to listen to others and take advice. When listening to others and accepting advice, the attitude we have when doing so is one of reconciliation. It may be reconciliation with the person giving advice, or it may be that the person we are listening to is providing wisdom that will help us reconcile with another person or with God. There are other serious ramifications of pride. In the book of Psalms, chapter 10, verse 4, God tells us that, "In his pride the wicked man does not seek the Lord; in all his thoughts there is no room for God." Pride keeps a person in bondage to their own selfish feelings. It keeps people thinking they must first address their needs and wants before thinking of others. If a prideful person is focused on themselves, there is clearly no way they are focused on God. However, all is not lost. With the power of Agape love, pride can be broken. All that is needed is a willing heart. A person filled with pride needs to recognize the damage their pride is doing to their relationships and how pride prevents love from being abundant within their own soul. A prideful person needs to surrender to God and repent of their sin. A prideful person needs to relinquish the tendency to control other people because they think their way is always the best way or only way. A prideful person needs to put others ahead of themselves. The only way to make the changes needed to remove prideful thoughts and the associated behavior is to connect with God and allow the flow of His love to move through a person's soul. Prideful thoughts are defeated by His love because when we love others we think of them before ourselves.

Whether the hurdle to reconciliation with another person is lack of honesty, transparency, trust, or our pride, there is another important facet of achieving reconciliation. People approach reconciliation as an event, such as when someone asks to sit down and have a conversation to resolve tension between themselves and another person. Reconciliation is much more than a one-time event. The initial discussion in an attempt to reconcile with someone is only the first step. When this discussion happens and there is a true meeting of the minds, genuine heartfelt apologies are exchanged, asking for and receiving forgiveness occurs, and most people feel much better as described earlier. However, lasting reconciliation includes choosing to forget about the past and loving the other person consistently and continuously. We have discussed loving others at length in this book. The love, of course, is Agape love. Forgetting the past wrongs people have done to us is not easy, but needed. We can use how God treats our sins as an example. In the book of Hebrews, chapter 8, verse 12, God says, "For I will be merciful toward their iniquities, and I will remember their sins no more." In the book of Jeremiah, chapter 31, verse 34, God says, "For I will forgive their wickedness and will remember their sins no more." In the book of Psalms, chapter 103, verse 12, God says, "as far as the east is from the west, so far has He removed our transgressions from us." In the book of Isaiah, chapter 43, verse 25, God says, "I, even, I, am He who blots out your transgressions, for my own sake, and remembers your sins no more." There are many more verses of scripture on this subject, but the scripture quoted here clearly show that God remembers our sins no more. Please keep in mind that the prerequisite or means of activating God's forgiveness and Him remembering our sins no more is for us to repent and ask for forgiveness. One particular verse, Psalm 103, verse 12 contains an explicit description of God forgetting our sins as He states that He will remove our sins as far as the east is from the west. Think about that. Where do the east and west begin and end? We think of those as directions, as are north and south. However, north and south clearly have start and finish points. Those points are the North Pole and the South Pole. When you are standing on the North Pole, every step you take is heading south. It could be southeast or southwest, but it is still south. When you are standing on the South Pole, every step you take is heading north. It could be northeast or northwest, but it is still north. East and west do not have start and finish points. You can conclude that God's forgiveness never ends, or said another way, is infinite.

True and lasting reconciliation involves repentance, asking for forgiveness, and forgetting the wrongs done to us or other people forgetting the wrongs we did to them. Lasting reconciliation is not an event, but a continued practice of a lifestyle of love.

Before we close this chapter and leave the subject of reconciliation, there is one more significant difference between reconciliation with God and reconciliation with people other than God. For example, if we had a disagreement with someone, and the cause of the disagreement was that we did not share the same opinion on a social issue, we could achieve reconciliation even though our opinions on the social issue differ. The reconciliation would be based upon listening to the person and attempting to understand why they think the way they think on the social issue that is in dispute. In addition, when we approach the person with whom we have an issue that we do not see eye to eye with in love, we are more adequately prepared to have patience and successfully begin to understand why they think the way they do. We will be more willing to accept the fact that the perspective and opinion the person has regarding the social issue is clearly owned by them and they have the right to own any opinion, even if we view that opinion as inaccurate.

We must accept the fact that our difference of opinion can have three outcomes. Either the opinions of both people are wrong or one of the two people holds an opinion that is wrong and the other person's opinion is correct, or visa-versa. If the latter is the case, there is uncertainty regarding who is correct. With enough effort, the two people can come to the conclusion that one of them holds an opinion that is correct. That can be a by-product of reconciling. However, it is more likely that there will not be an agreement regarding who is correct. The two people can agree that their perspectives are different but that does not mean that those differences will keep the two people from loving each other and reconciling.

The difference between reconciling with another person due to a disagreement based upon different perspectives and reconciling with God is explained by who He is. Since God is perfect, His opinion is always correct because it is truth. We must agree with Him to reconcile because God is not going to reconcile or agree with us when we do not acknowledge the truth. Agreeing with Him is a good thing inasmuch as we are agreeing with a perspective that is true. An example may help demonstrate one way we benefit. Let's assume you studied spiders and could easily recognize spiders that are harmful versus spiders that are harmless. If I realize that you have wisdom regarding spiders and I listen to, and act upon, your knowledge, it will benefit me tremendously. This is particularly true if I encounter a spider that is harmful. In the same way, God knows all including knowing what is harmful to us and what is good for us. We benefit greatly by listening to God's wisdom and seeking to understand what He tells us. Agreeing with God is easy to do if we are cognizant of His holiness, righteousness, goodness, and wisdom.

We can reconcile with God but not fully understand God. The complexities of creation are such that we may never understand how God created the universe, or us. That does not preclude us from reconciling with Him. We must trust Him and never stop seeking to understand what He has to say to us, knowing what He has to say is of great value to us. There is no better scripture than Proverbs, chapter 3, verse 5 to describe this concept. The verse read, "Trust in the Lord with all your heart, and lean not on your own understanding." The Hebrew word used for the word trust in verse 5 is batach, which is a verb indicating to trust; to be confident. We are confidently trusting God. That confidence stems from being able to rely on the person we trust; in this case, God, who is perfect. The phrase "all your heart" makes it clear that every part of our being should trust God. The Hebrew word used for the word understanding in verse 5 is biynah, which is a noun meaning discernment, comprehension, and understanding. While God has given us the ability to think and comprehend, we are imperfect and need God to provide wisdom that comes from deep understanding as we think through the various truths of life. This can only be accomplished if we trust God and diligently seek to understand the truths He has given us. God simultaneously and periodically provides wisdom if we ask and while we are in the midst of seeking understanding.

What are the benefits of reconciling with God? We have already touched upon a few of these benefits throughout this book. We are filled with peace versus living in a state of spiritual tension. There is spiritual order governing our lives versus chaos. There is stability versus uncertainty. There is true joy versus a lack of joy. There is the inheritance of eternal life versus never seeing God nor partaking in all that He wants for us. Eternal life is often misunderstood and, in extreme cases, is not believed to exist. Some people believe when their physical bodies die, there is no more existence. On the other hand, there are folks who believe that when their physical bodies die, their soul travels to another place. There are significant differences in those views. Given the massive importance to each of us, the concept of eternal life and what occurs after our physical bodies die is worthy of thorough contemplation.

Therefore, we have dedicated the next chapter to a discussion of the truth regarding eternal life.

CHAPTER 11

Life After Physical Death Occurs

Physical death can occur at any moment and in a multitude of ways. Perhaps physical death is something you do not spend much time thinking about. After all, few people look forward to the moment when their heart beats for the last time. Virtually all human beings, other than very young children, are aware that physical death is inevitable. Many adults plan for their death. They prepare a will so that their wishes regarding the disposition of any assets accumulated during their lifetime is carried out. They also make decisions about what will happen to their physical body. Even though physical death may be planned for, it is still not an event many look forward to. Woody Allen was credited with saying something that most of us feel when he said, "I'm not afraid to die. I just don't want to be there when it happens." We tend to not want to dwell on physical death because there is perceived potential significant pain and suffering that can occur during the process. However, even though we typically avoid thinking about the process of our physical bodies dying, there is an innate curiosity regarding what happens immediately following the moment our physical body dies. There are many opinions about what happens to us when our physical bodies die. We will not address every opinion, but will discuss the opinions collectively in categories and drill down deeper on each category for clarification of the truth.

The three categories of opinions to be addressed are:

- those who believe that when our physical bodies die, we no longer exist
- those who believe that when our physical bodies die, our soul is reincarnated into another physical living thing
- those who believe that when our physical bodies die, our soul fully enters the spiritual realm unencumbered by attachment to a physical body.

People who hold the opinion of the first category mentioned above are solely focused on the physical realm. They essentially believe that what you see is all that exists. People who hold this opinion would tend to have no belief in God because a belief in God would cause an internal conflict of thought. The conflict would be caused by having to explain a God that they cannot see, but Whom has said He is always with us, which would imply a spiritual realm exists. In addition, believing in God would require attempting to understand what He has told us, almost all of which would contradict the belief that when our physical bodies die, we cease to exist. It is very likely that people who believe that when our physical bodies die we cease to exist do not believe in God.

What is the basis for holding the opinion that when our physical bodies die, we cease to exist? The fact that there is tangible evidence people have of everything they do in life, everything they see around them, and everything they have known to exist is a significant factor in forming the opinion of ceasing to exist after our physical bodies die. If this is the sole basis for the ceasing to exist after physical death opinion, people should consider that holding a view that there is a spiritual realm does not preclude belief in everything in the physical realm. Furthermore, much of what is taught to us by pursuing an understanding of the spiritual realm helps explain the physical realm. God reveals in scripture how we began, why we began, and what happens when our physical bodies die. Of course, to accept what God has told us there must first be a belief that God exists. A person who does not believe God exists should explore the physical and supernatural evidence of whether or not God exists. There is overwhelming evidence of His existence when approached impartially. In chapter 1 we discussed various factors that shape a person's beliefs. These factors are can create opinions that are solidified in a person's mind over time even if those opinions are incorrect. For example, we have had an intense focus recently in the United States regarding one particular type of altercation leading to injury or death. That type of altercation is between police officers and civilians. These altercations begin with a call for help to the police or the police witnessing a potentially criminal situation in progress. There are presuppositions made about what happened in each case, typically before the facts are known. There are assumptions and rushes to judgement, which are influenced by a world view or perspective that existed before the event occurred. The pre-existing perspective was formed over time through listening to various opinions and making decisions to form an opinion based upon what was heard, not necessarily the facts. That does not mean that there have not been cases of real police mistreatment of people, however, it does mean that we should not extrapolate the circumstances of one event or repeated events to an entire population (in this case all law enforcement officers in the United States).

The best course of action when reflecting upon events that occur in life is to try to understand all the facts before making a judgement about the event. When the facts are known, it is much easier to determine whether or not the actions of all parties in any given situation are noble. In other words, are the actions of the people involved motivated by good or evil intentions? Each event is unique as are the people involved. So why would we extrapolate a motive for a particular outcome and assign guilt or innocence simply based upon what happened last time a similar event took place. The advice regarding gathering facts before making judgements about situations or forming beliefs about almost every event or subject is promulgated by God. In the book of Proverbs, chapter 14, verse 29, God says, "Whoever is patient has great understanding, but one who is quick-tempered displays folly." Gathering facts takes patience. Patience to set our emotions aside. When we are able to be patient, we preserve the peace God promises while we are gaining insight and understanding.

It is very difficult for many people who hold a strong belief to listen to facts that prove what they believe may be wrong. This is because we all think within a framework of what we already believe and make the assumption that what we already believe must be true because it is what we believe. However, our opinions can, and often do, change as we gain more understanding. In the case of the folks who only believe in the physical realm, if they are presented with enough evidence of the existence of a spiritual realm, and they earnestly seek to understand more, they can be persuaded to change their view. The same applies to almost any view on almost any subject.

The perspective that only the physical exists deserves much more discussion. If a person who holds this view works backward in time, they will be faced with a dilemma. The basis for holding the view that the physical is all that exists cannot be applied retroactively throughout the existence of humanity. Attempting to do so is applying a theory that cannot be proved. To elaborate, we can agree that there is a definite beginning to our physical bodies. That beginning happened at conception. There were two other physical people involved in bringing about our conception. Those two other people also had a definite beginning to their physical bodies. That beginning occurred in the same way their offspring were created. As you think in reverse chronological order in this manner, a person who believes that only the physical exists must find a way to explain how this initially began. Since it is likely that most people who believe only the physical exists do not believe in God, they cannot attribute the beginning to God. So, they believe the beginning took place through one of various theories, the most common explains the beginning as a large cosmic explosion where hundreds of protein molecules came together to create life by random connection. The belief in a random event that started all life as we know it does help the person who does not want to attribute the creation of life to God. However, belief in the type of event described does not preclude a person from believing in God. Hence, there are folks who believe in God and attribute the seemingly random event of creation to having been initiated by God. For this person who believes that what is physical is all there is and believes in God they must also believe God is only physical and, therefore, there is no spiritual nature to God. To believe that God is more than just a physical being would contradict their theory that the physical is all that exists, which would render the latter opinion invalid.

The truth regarding spiritual forces is documented in chapter 2 of this book. If there is anyone who believes the physical is all that exists and is reading this book, I would urge them to use an impartial approach to assessing the information presented regarding the spiritual realm. If you accept the idea that a spiritual dimension exists, and from the spiritual dimension human beings are tempted to sin, and are also empowered to overcome sin, all that needs to be linked within your mind is that the temptations from a spiritual dimension tempt something in the same dimension. When a human is tempted, their soul receives the temptation. If that human, who is tempted, then sins in the physical, it is because the soul, which is spiritual, resides within the physical body. Our physical body acts upon the promptings from our soul. This is why God tells us in the book of Proverbs, chapter 4, verse 23 to "Above all else, guard your heart, for everything you do flows from it." The heart is our soul. God tells us to guard our soul from temptation. He knows that if the soul cannot withstand the urge to sin stemming from temptation, the sin will occur in the physical. Conversely, if we detect temptation quickly and take action to shut down the temptation while operating in the spiritual, there will be no influence of the temptation of our soul on our physical being. Hence, we will have victory over sin. The key is to make the pattern of thought and behavior that led to subduing sin habitual and engrained in our thinking, which begins with our spiritual being. You can sin in both the spiritual realm and the physical realm. You can sin in only the spiritual realm. You cannot sin in the physical realm without sinning in the spiritual realm. A simpler way to think about this is a thought occurs before an action.

Our hope is that you can see the danger in thinking there is no spiritual realm; in other words, thinking the physical realm is the only existence. The greatest danger is to miss living a life of obedience to God and missing out on eternity with Him. The second danger for a person who believes only the physical exists is becoming susceptible to temptation because it is not possible to defend oneself if the spiritual dimension is not acknowledged. These two dangers are intertwined. During our discussion earlier in the book, the truth regarding temptation and how to defeat sin was established as a battle in the spiritual dimension.

Let's move on to the next category of beliefs regarding life after death. The second category is composed of those who believe that when our physical bodies die, our spiritual being travels through the spiritual dimension until our spiritual being is assigned another physical living thing to become its' next home. This category has some complex as well as conflicting thinking. For example, some folks believe that God orchestrates the assignment of the spirit being its' next destination and some folks in this category do not believe God makes the assignment but rather a process in place that is naturally predesigned. Regardless of whether people in this category attribute the next destination of our spirit being to a decision by God or not, most believe that their own behavior is the factor that earns them (positively or negatively) where they go next. Hence, either God weighs how a person lived their life in deciding where their spirit goes next or some cosmic predesigned process takes the totality of how a person lived their life and the person's spirit being is directed to its' next destination. The latter belief is similar to a law of physics applied to an action. In this case, though, the rewards or consequences of behavior are manifested in the reception of a new physical location for the spirit being.

There are many variations included in the category of belief that a person's spirit being leaves the body they currently occupy upon death and ultimately receives a new physical home. In fact, there are so many variations that many books have been written on the subject and organizations formed with vast followers.

The questions every human being should ask themselves before accepting any philosophy as truth is, "What is the basis for the belief?" and "What evidence exists to validate the belief?" As a general rule, a person telling you that you cannot disprove their belief does not make the belief true. Nor is it effective in persuading others that the belief is true. In addition, since the matters of life after death have potentially serious ramifications, we owe it to ourselves to explore this particular matter deeply and obtain evidence to identify the truth.

Many folks accept a belief because they become enamored with the concept, but fail to thoroughly examine whether or not the belief is indeed true. All truth can be proven. Often, the proof is physical. Sometimes, the proof is spiritual. The primary message being communicated here is the strong recommendation to have some form of proof before latching on to a belief. To do otherwise does a disservice to oneself and others whom you may share your belief with that is not truth. The concepts being identified as truth in this book have always included either physical or spiritual evidence supporting the truth. Our hope is that the reader will spend time contemplating the support provided if the specific truth being supported is a truth that was not embraced by the reader prior to reading this book. Skepticism can be a very good thing if the person who is skeptical of a certain truth is being intellectually honest with themselves and unbiased by preconceived notions. The underlying point is if a person holds an opinion or belief that is untrue, that person will have difficulty comprehending and beginning to believe the truth because the opinion they have causes them to see the truth in a biased manner. Since the truth will contradict the untruth that a person may already believe, holding on to a belief that is untrue will preclude them from seeing the truth as truth. A belief in an untruth will generate a natural bias against believing the truth because the individual believes in an untruth. Let's look at an example of this concept. On January 19, 1977 the State of Florida experienced the only known snowfall to have occurred. If you did not live in the State of Florida on January 19, 1977 but happened to be visiting the State of Florida, and had no other knowledge of Florida's climate, you would believe that snowfall is normal during the winter in Florida. If you did not conduct research to determine whether or not your belief is true, you may continue to believe that snowfall in Florida is normal. If you mentioned your belief to someone who then told you that you happened to be in Florida the only day it has ever snowed there, you would be skeptical. If that skepticism led you to do some research you would find the truth and, subsequent to learning the truth, change your belief.

The same process of identifying the truth and altering an opinion or belief from an untruth to the truth that we saw in the snowfall in Florida example can be applied to the understanding of truth versus untruth for any subject. The extent of effort put forth to find the truth may vary proportionately with how important knowing the truth for a particular subject is to us or how curious we are to know more about a particular subject. If, for example, you have a strong desire to know how bees produce honey, you will likely put forth effort to understand the truths related to the production of honey. You may also attempt to understand the truth regarding the health benefits of honey. Your desire to understand the truth is fueled by curiosity or a belief that it may be very important to understand the truth about this subject. On the other hand, if you have no desire to understand the truth about, for example, why hot air balloons float in the air, it is likely you are not curious about the subject of hot air balloons nor believe there is any importance in your life attached to knowing why hot air balloons float in the air. Not desiring to know the truth about a particular subject is typically a lack of interest in that subject. If that is the case, there is generally no significant impact to a person's life for being disinterested in a specific subject. However, there are necessarily negative ramifications to a person's life of not desiring to pursue the truth about a certain subject if you have a strong desire to know the truth and you currently believe you already know the truth, however, what you believe is the truth is not the truth. The most extreme negative ramifications come to fruition in the case of a person believing that God does not exist when, in fact, the truth is God does exist.

You can apply the line of thinking regarding pursuing or not pursuing the truth to any subject. You can also learn much about a person by understanding what subjects they desire to know truth and what subjects they do not desire to know truth.

The third category of opinions is composed of those who believe that when our physical bodies die, our soul fully enters the spiritual realm unencumbered by attachment to a physical body. Much evidence is available and will be used to support this category of opinions. In doing so, we will learn that there are many variations of the general concept of this third opinion category. As we have often learned in life, though, there is only one truth. To build a deep, thorough understanding of the truth regarding what happens when our physical bodies die, we will walk through a few verses of scripture. The first verse is found in the book of Isaiah, chapter 25, verse 8. God tells us in the first part of this verse that, "He will swallow up death forever." In this verse, death refers to the fact that we will neither have to experience physical death more than once nor experience spiritual death at all. The reason is the Messiah, Jesus Christ, came to earth and He died and rose from the dead to defeat sin and death. There is an irrefutable fact that the physical body we now occupy will die. Isaiah cannot be talking about that death in as much as death is removed forever. He is talking about life beyond the passing of our physical body. The next verse is the most quoted verse of the past couple of generations. The verse is found in the book of John, chapter 3, verse 16, which reads, "For God so loved the world that He gave His one and only Son, that whoever believes in Him shall not perish but have eternal life." Once again, we know the physical body dies, but God is saying if we believe we will not perish. The reference can only be to our spirit being. The soul will not have to die and will live forever as long as we believe that Jesus Christ is God and our Savior. Sounds like something every human would want. In the book of Philippians, chapter 1, verse 21, God tells us that, "To live is Christ and to die is gain." If we live our lives not only with the belief that

Jesus Christ is our Savior, but by obeying His commands, our physical bodies will still die. However, our spirit will gain. What will our spirit gain? That is a question with a multi-faceted answer. Before dissecting the answer into easily digestible segments, it should be noted that something wonderful is going to happen to our soul after we take our last breath physically. What we gain means that we acquire something that we do not possess today. From the previous two verses, we know that we gain eternal life. Eternal life means in whatever manner our spirit being is living, it will be ongoing forever. There will be no end. Never again will we be bound by managing our life in finite time periods. Today, we are considered children if we are under the age of eighteen. Between the ages of eighteen and thirty-five we are considered young adults. Between the ages of thirty-five and sixty-five we are considered middle aged adults. Finally, if we are over the age of sixty-five we are considered elderly. These are arbitrary time segments but are cited to illustrate a point. The point is that as we live our lives we are cognizant of which time period we live in and understand there are certain norms associated with each time period. Many people strive to live according to the cultural norms that exist for each time period. There is nothing wrong with that, and, in fact, is practical. However, doing so makes people tend to think of their lives as limited, or finite. Of course, there is a limited time period for our physical bodies, but the time constraint of living within a physical body is not applicable to eternal life, as there is only one time period, which is endless. Therefore, from an eternal perspective there is no need for managing how we live as we age given we are blessed with unending time. That alone is cause to feel great joy! In addition, the type of mindset we have as we live life in a physical body will determine how well we live life when we depart our physical body and influence how we spend eternity.

In chapter 10 we spent much time determining how to reconcile with God and the benefits of that reconciliation. Those benefits include eternal life with God. We want to elaborate on those benefits as they accrue to us after our physical bodies perish, which is the focus of this chapter. There are many verses of scripture that address heaven. Let's begin with the book of Exodus, chapter 20 verse 22. The verse reads, "Then the Lord said to Moses, Tell the Israelites this: You have seen for yourselves that I have spoken to you from heaven." In the book of Deuteronomy, chapter 26, verse 15 God shows us more evidence of whom resides in heaven, "Look down from heaven, your holy dwelling place, and bless your people Israel and the land you have given us as you promised on oath to our forefathers, a land flowing with milk and honey." The word heaven used here is the Hebrew word, shamayim. The meaning of this word as used here refers to the sky and as far as we can see. Humans living in our physical bodies typically do not have the ability to see heaven, but it is consistently described as a place far away from the earth. These verses are telling us where God resides. In the book of Daniel, chapter 2, the first part of verse 28, God tells us, "but there is a God in heaven who reveals mysteries." The Hebrew word used here for heaven is shmayin; the meaning is very similar to the word shamayim, but has a different connotation. Shmayin means the dwelling place of God that is much higher than any other place. The word shmayin is meant to emphasize the point that heaven is far from us and is a holy place given God is there. In the book of Isaiah, chapter 66, verse 1, the word shamayim is used. This verse is, "Thus says the Lord: Heaven is my throne, and the earth is my footstool; what is the house that you would build for me, and what is the place of my rest?" God is explaining to us how big He is to assist us in understanding who we are in comparison to Him. What we can conclude thus far is that heaven is a vast domain, God is present there, and we have to travel in some manner to get there.

How do we know our spirit is going to a place called heaven? First, we are not guaranteed to go to heaven, but we will return to that matter in a moment. In the book of Matthew, chapter 3, verse 2, God tells us to, "Repent, for the kingdom of heaven is at hand." This verse is clearly telling us that our next destination can be heaven if we repent. The book of 2 Corinthians, chapter 5, verses 8-9 read, "We are confident I say, and would prefer to be away from the body and at home with the Lord. So we make it our goal to please Him, whether we are at home in the body or away from it." These verses indicate that our spirit can dwell in our physical bodies or not. In the same book (2 Corinthians), and the same chapter (5), verse 1 states that, "Now we know that if the earthly tent we live in is destroyed, we have a building from God, an eternal house in heaven, not built by human hands." Our earthly tent is our physical body. Again, this is just more support that once we leave our physical body, we will dwell somewhere else, and that somewhere else is heaven.

Knowing that there is a heaven, that God lives there, and that we can be there too is great to understand, however, we also need to be aware of, and do, what God asks of us to ensure we go to heaven after we take our last breath on earth. We have learned that repentance is required to go to heaven. It is repentance accompanied by a commitment to change our ways. Our new way of living consists of listening to what God asks us each day and doing what He asks, which is essentially turning away from any behavior that is sinful and replace it with love. In the book of Matthew, chapter 7, verses 21-23 we read, "Not everyone who says to me, Lord, Lord will enter the kingdom of heaven, but only he who does the will of my father who is in heaven." In other words, you cannot con God! God knows our every thought. Documented in scripture are a few examples of people whom hid the truth from God. One of the examples that demonstrates how lying to God will prevent us from entering the kingdom of heaven is the detailed account of Ananias and Sapphira. The account is written in the book of Acts, chapter 5, verses 1-11. The scripture reads, "Now a man named Ananias, together with his wife Sapphira, also sold a piece of property. With his wife's full knowledge he kept back part of the money for himself, but brought the rest and put it at the apostles' feet.

Then Peter said, 'Ananias, how is it that Satan has so filled your heart that you have lied to the Holy Spirit and have kept for yourself some of the money you received for the land? Didn't it belong to you before it was sold? And after it was sold, wasn't the money at your disposal? What made you think of doing such a thing? You have not lied just to human beings but to God.' When Ananias heard this, he fell down and died. And great fear seized all who heard what had happened. Then some young men came forward, wrapped up his body, and carried him out and buried him. About three hours later his wife came in, not knowing what had happened. Peter asked her, 'Tell me, is this the price you and Ananias got for the land?' 'Yes,' she said, 'that is the price.' Peter said to her, 'How could you conspire to test the Spirit of the Lord? Listen! The feet of the men who buried your husband are at the door, and they will carry you out also.'

At that moment she fell down at his feet and died. Then the young men came in and, finding her dead, carried her out and buried her beside her husband. Great fear seized the whole church and all who heard about these events." Obviously Ananias and Sapphira succumbed to the temptation of the love of money manifested in greed. Note that Ananias and Sapphira may have had the right to keep a portion of the money they received when they sold their land, however, they were not forthright and honest about their desire, so they lied about what they did. The result for them was catastrophic.

Given the warning in Matthew, chapter 7, verses 21-23 cited above, what do we need to do to assure ourselves of eternal life? If we confess with our mouths that Jesus Christ is God and we acknowledge what He did for us through His crucifixion and subsequent resurrection thereby accepting the gift of salvation through Him and we turn from our previous sinful ways, then, and only then, will we be on the path toward achieving our heavenly reward. Furthermore, consistent focus on what God has told us will empower us to utilize the power of God's Holy Spirit to defeat sin in our lives.

Is the reward for obedience and faith simply eternal life in heaven? Or, are the rewards for those who do go to heaven of varying degrees based upon other factors? These questions have been debated by Christians for a long time. Some believe that the reward is eternal life. A scripture that seems to address this belief is found in the book of Matthew, chapter 20, verses 1-15. This scripture is a parable about a vineyard. Some workers start early and work a full day, some come later in the day. Regardless of how many hours worked, each laborer receives the same pay. The reward (or pay) is clearly analogous to the kingdom of heaven. Is the reward just being able to make it to heaven or is the reward representing what we receive once we are in heaven? There are several other scripture that can help us answer this question. In the book of Matthew, chapter 5, verses 11-12, God tells us, "Blessed are you when men cast insults at you, and persecute you, and say all kinds of evil against you falsely, on account of Me. Rejoice, and be glad, for your reward in heaven is great, for so they persecuted the prophets who were before you." God is telling us that the kingdom of heaven will be great, but your rewards once you arrive will be much if you face persecution of various kinds while on earth. In the book of Matthew, chapter 6, God tells us that heavenly rewards will be given in proportion to the degree we are obedient to God's commands and based upon the amount of His will we participate in while on earth. The more we pursue holiness and love God and others, the greater the rewards in heaven. Furthermore, He tells us in verse 20 to store up treasures in heaven rather than on earth, emphasizing that heavenly rewards are far better than anything we can obtain while on earth. If we think about the fact that heavenly rewards are better than earthly fortune and that heavenly rewards are eternal, that should motivate us to do whatever we can to maximize heavenly rewards. Another scripture related to this subject is found in the book of Matthew, chapter 16, verse 27, where God says, "For the Son of Man is going to come in the glory of His Father with His angels; and will then recompense every man according to his deeds." This scripture is spoken by Jesus and He is telling us that God is fair and just and will give rewards to us in heaven according to what we have done before we get to heaven. If you are not convinced yet that God will give varying degrees of rewards, please refer to a passage of scripture in Matthew, chapter 25, verses 14-30. There are several other scripture passages that corroborate this line of thinking including the book of 2 John, verses 4-10. In the passage from 2 John, God is encouraging us to work hard to receive a full reward. It is implied that some will receive a partial reward when they get to heaven. A partial reward in heaven is still infinitely better than anything we could experience or receive on earth, but God is encouraging us to give our best each day on earth by explaining the magnitude of rewards in heaven. There is really no effective analogy on earth to heavenly rewards, however, here is an attempt to cite one. Let's say you were given airline flight tickets to Hawaii and hotel accommodations. Most people would be extremely excited upon learning of their gift. As a side note, we should feel a much greater level of excitement knowing we have received the gift of salvation and our eternal destination is heaven as compared to the feeling we experience upon learning we are going to Hawaii. Let's get back to the Hawaiian vacation. Once we arrive in Hawaii, we travel to our hotel. Some will stay at a luxury resort with many amenities. Some will stay at a lower budget hotel with few amenities. In either case, just being in Hawaii is a wonderful experience. However, the folks staying at the luxury resort will enjoy the extra benefits during their Hawaiian vacation. The same could be said for heaven. Everyone who goes to heaven will be filled with unlimited joy forever. God will give some more rewards while in heaven. The difference in rewards does not alter the fact that eternity is being spent in heaven, but earning the additional rewards can only enhance the experience. We are not provided enough insight to know the nature of heavenly rewards, but what we do know is we will be in a perfect place with no evil, no disease or sickness, perfect peace, and unimaginable joy. We will see things we have never seen before. We will be thankful continuously and praise God for what He has done. In the book of Revelation, chapter 7, verse 15-17 we see a partial description of heaven. It reads, "Therefore they are before the throne of God, and serve Him day and night in His temple. And He who sits on the throne will dwell among them. They shall neither hunger anymore nor thirst anymore; the sun shall not strike them, nor any heat; for the Lamb who is in the midst of the throne will shepherd them and lead them to living fountains of waters. And God will wipe away every tear from their eyes." Another description is found in the book of Revelation, chapter 21, verses 9-11. There are several other scripture that clearly point to the fact that heaven will be a beautiful place, and a place we can hardly imagine. Jesus called heaven "paradise" in the book of Luke, chapter 23, verse 43. In the book of Revelation, chapter 21, verse 21 heaven is described as, "The twelve gates were twelve pearls: each gate made of a single pearl. And the great street of the city was pure gold, like transparent glass."

We have learned what heaven is, who resides there, how we can get there, and a bit about what heaven is like. What we learned thus far refers to heaven as it exists today. The realization of what we have learned thus far about heaven should be enough to generate enormous excitement about our future and motivate us to repent for what we have done and be obedient to what God asks of us. However, there is even more good news. Heaven as it exists today is not heaven as it will be forever. It becomes even better! You should ask, "How can a perfect place become better?" By definition, something that is perfect has no room for improvement. Let's explore why we can say that heaven in the future will be better than heaven today. First, let's look at the book of Revelation, chapter 21, verses 1 and 2. In this passage of scripture, God tells us, "Then I saw a new heaven and a new earth, for the first heaven and the first earth had passed away, and there was no longer any sea. I saw the Holy City, the new Jerusalem, coming down out of heaven from God, prepared as a bride beautifully dressed for her husband." The description in this passage indicates that God will create a new Jerusalem that will become the Holy City located in the new heaven. The new heaven will be located upon the new earth. In addition, it is revealed to us through this scripture that the current heaven and earth shall pass away, or cease to exist. These new existences are referred to the book of Hebrews, chapter 12, verse 22, which states, "But you have come to Mount Zion, the heavenly Jerusalem, the city of the living God. You have come to thousands upon thousands of angels in joyful assembly." This verse clearly refers to the new Jerusalem in the new heaven, and it is a place where God lives. Jerusalem is often call Zion. Mount Zion is the place where the fortress of the city of Jerusalem was built. Jerusalem is a holy city for people of Jewish, Christian, and Muslim faiths. The name Jerusalem means "city of peace." All of these facts are consistent with the importance of the city of Jerusalem and the idea that God will create a new Jerusalem. The timing of the creation of the new Jerusalem is not fully understood but can be placed between milestone events in the future. Those events are often debated in terms of the timing, but not the fact that they will occur. Rather than focus on the substance of the debate over the timing of these events, suffice it to say that God tells us these events will come to pass and the timing is not as important as the fact that a new Jerusalem will be created in the new heaven.

Furthermore, in the book of Isaiah, chapter 65, verses 17-19, God tells us, "Behold, I will create new heavens and a new earth. The former things will not be remembered, nor will they come to mind. But, be glad and rejoice forever in what I will create, for I will create Jerusalem to be a delight, and its' people a joy. I will rejoice in Jerusalem and take delight in my people; the sound of weeping and crying will be heard in it no more." Sounds like a place anyone would want to spend eternity. There will be no weeping or crying, but only joy. God tells us these things to show us how much He loves us and what we have to look forward to. In addition, this information about us spending an eternity in a perfect place absent of evil, sickness, sadness and, instead, filled with peace and joy should be sufficient motivation to live for God during our time on earth. However, many are deceived into living selfishly while on earth and, ultimately, do not get to enjoy what God has intended for every one of His children. There is one other point that is alluded to in this passage. If God creates a new Jerusalem in a new heaven, why does He also create a new earth? No one knows for certain, but many Bible scholars believe the new Jerusalem in the new heaven is on the new earth. The renewed earth would be the perfect place for us to live forever. It also is the place that adds a physical dimension in addition to the spiritual dimension. That implies that we will be given another physical body for our spirit being to reside in. There are several scripture that corroborate that implication. Those scripture include Isaiah 26:19-21 and 1 Thessalonians 4:13-17. There are entire books written on the subject of the resurrection of the dead and the events that will occur after the judgement of all people by God. We are merely covering a macro view of what happens to us, not all the events of what will occur before the new Jerusalem in the new heaven on the new earth is established. What is shared here is intended to provide an overview and be encouragement for those who desire to know what is to come for a believer. Or, if an unbeliever has enough proof, such as what is being offered in this chapter, they may come to an understanding of the truth and be convinced of the truth. If that happens, there is a natural inclination to accept the truth and then the truth becomes part of the person's world view. When the individual's world view changes and the acknowledgement of truth becomes part of the change, a person's life is impacted in a powerful way forever.

In this chapter we have covered a lot of ground regarding the types of beliefs people possess about life after death. The truth shared has been all positive in terms of what we can experience. However, it would be a mistake to avoid a discussion of the negative aspect of life after death. The negative side is essentially the punishment that a human being will receive for living a life of disobedience to God or not acknowledging that He exists. As we have all experienced, there are consequences for our actions. Typically, anything we do while on earth will either earn us a blessing of eternal life or a consequence. Those consequences will occur while on earth or after we take our last breath. For example, if you are driving over the speed limit, it is likely you will be pulled over by a police officer and given a much deserved citation. A second example is if we do not take care of our physical bodies, our physical life will be shortened. A third example is if we do not discipline our children and teach them right from wrong, they will tend to be unruly and disobedient children. The list of consequences that we may experience while on earth is endless. However, the fact is that there are consequences we will not experience until after our physical bodies perish. These consequences are punishment for actions that took place during our time on earth while in our physical bodies. So, what if we do not make it to heaven? What does a person's eternity look like then? These questions are not for the weak of heart. Taking time to answer them makes us confront the reality of a future based upon failing to obey God's commands. So, let's take a deeper look at the punishment that awaits a person who disobeys God.

One of the most common questions people ask is, "Why would a God who loves us punish us so severely?" The answer is that God is perfect, which would make Him perfectly fair. If you were in school and studied very hard and scored a 98% on a test you would expect an

"A" for a grade. If another student did not study and scored a 49% on the same test, you would expect that student would receive an 'F" for a grade. If, however, the teacher decided every student would receive an "A" regardless of their score on the test, you would conclude that the teacher is not being fair...and, you would be correct. God, being perfect, can only be fair. To be otherwise would be an imperfection. Therefore, the disobedient receive punishment while the obedient receive rewards. In the book of Proverbs, chapter 2, verses 7-9, God tells us that, "He holds victory in store for the upright, He is a shield to those whose walk is blameless, for He guards the course of the just and protects the way of His faithful ones. Then you will understand what is right and just and fair---every good path." God loves us so much that He wants to do what is stated in these verses in Proverbs. As He does, we begin to understand what is right and just and fair. Obedience should be rewarded. Conversely, disobedience earns consequences. Those last two thoughts constitute fairness. As we will see, God makes clear the consequences of disobedience. In the book of Exodus, chapter 32, verses 33-34 God tells us, "The Lord replied to Moses, Whoever has sinned against Me I will blot out of My book. Now go, lead the people to the place I spoke of, and My angel will go before you. However, when the time comes for me to punish, I will punish them for their sin." Here we see strong evidence of God's intention to punish people for their disobedience.

Some people use human emotions to explain God's behavior or change what He says because it doesn't "feel right" to them. For example, I have heard people say that if God is perfect, He cannot experience anger. They "feel" anger is an imperfection. There are times anger is perfectly appropriate and justified and does not in any way take away from holiness. However, the times it is appropriate are justified by extreme circumstances. Anger is not justified because someone gossips about you, but it is justified when someone you love is murdered. At this point in the book, you should be able to see the difference between those circumstances. In both cases, we are called to forgive, however, in the latter case we still expect punishment to be rendered for the crime committed.

Whether or not we believe God's intention to reward and punish is fair, it is a fact. We would be foolish to ignore the facts or somehow convince ourselves that disobedience is not going to be punished because "God is a loving God", which is another mantra many people recite when discussing this subject. Of course God is loving as that is Who He is. Love and fairness are completely compatible; as are rewards and punishment. Most parents understand this. While we love our children, we also reward good behavior (obedience) and punish bad behavior (disobedience). Fairness is apparent when parents consistently reward and punish appropriately. God loves fairness and abhors injustice. In the book of Proverbs, chapter 17, verse 15, God tells us that, "Acquitting the guilty and condemning the innocent – the Lord detests them both."

Evidence of God's intent to punish is found in the book of Isaiah, chapter 13, verse 11 where God says, "I will punish the world for its' evil, the wicked for their sins." In the book of Jeremiah, chapter 4, verse 18, God tells us that, "Your own conduct and actions have brought this upon you. This is your punishment." In the book of Jeremiah, chapter 21, verse 14 God tells us that, "I will punish you as your deeds deserve." Again in the book of Jeremiah, chapter 2, verse 19, God says, "Your wickedness will punish you, your backsliding will rebuke you. Consider then and realize how evil and bitter it is for you when you forsake the Lord your God and have no awe of Me, declares the Lord, the Lord Almighty." The book of 2 Thessalonians, chapter 1, verses 8-10 contain not only the fact that disobedience will be punished but provides more specific description of both the punishment for those who disobey and the rewards that await those who obey. Those verses say that, "He will punish those who do not know God and do not obey the gospel of our Lord Jesus. They will be punished with everlasting destruction and shut out from the presence of the Lord and from the glory of His might on the day He comes to be glorified in His holy people and to be marveled at among all those who have believed. This includes you, because you believed our testimony to you." This passage in the book of 2 Thessalonians should give any human who reads it reason to consider that, if what they are reading is true, there is no recovering from the punishment. Imagine the moment an unbeliever meets God and the realization that God exists becomes reality. It is impossible to know what the unbeliever would feel at that moment but it would not be a pleasant feeling. There is nothing on earth that is comparable but I will give you an example anyway. Let's assume you grew up and people told you that highway patrolmen and patrolwomen exist and that, if you drive over the speed limit, you would likely be pulled over and receive a speeding ticket. Let's further assume that you do not believe highway patrol personnel exist. One day you get on the highway and are in a bit of a hurry. You see flashing lights from a vehicle behind you and you are confronted with the realization that highway patrol personnel exist. You may not be afraid of what is about to happen but you will feel a bit upset. How much more upset would the unbeliever be or overcome with fear the moment the unbeliever confronts the reality of the living God?

This next scripture passage provides conclusive evidence that God administering punishment is consistent for disobedience, which is sin, while rescuing the righteous from punishment. The passage is found in 2 Peter chapter 2, verses 4-10. Here is the text from 2 Peter, "For if God did not spare angels when they sinned, but sent them to hell, putting them in chains of darkness to be held for judgment; if he did not spare the ancient world when he brought the flood on its ungodly people, but protected Noah, a preacher of righteousness, and seven others; if he condemned the cities of Sodom and Gomorrah by burning them to ashes, and made them an example of what is going to happen to the ungodly; and if he rescued Lot, a righteous man, who was distressed by the depraved conduct of the lawless (for that righteous man, living among them day after day, was tormented in his righteous soul by the lawless deeds he saw and heard)— if this is so, then the Lord knows how to rescue the godly from trials and to hold the unrighteous for punishment on the day of judgment. This is especially true of those who follow the corrupt desire of the flesh and despise authority."

You can clearly see from many of these scriptures regarding punishment that a person's behavior earns punishment. Before exploring specific punishment that awaits those who disobey, never lose sight of the fact that we all have a chance to repent from our disobedience (sin) and receive forgiveness. In other words, punishment for disobedience is guaranteed for those who hold no remorse for their sins against God, but can be avoided by a soul filled with an attitude of repentance that takes action to seek forgiveness and turn from their sinful ways. The last scripture presented (2 Peter) mentions that God can "rescue the godly from trials." Not only can God rescue the godly, He earnestly desires to. Remember what we learned about God's will in chapter 8? His will is that no one would perish. He loves each of us so much and hates the fact that many will not spend eternity with Him.

How will the punishment be carried out? The next few pages of the book comprise the most unpleasant part. One of the verses we already looked at in this chapter does describe punishment in part. In the book of 2 Thessalonians, chapter 1, verse 9 God tells us that, "They will be punished with everlasting destruction and shut out from the presence of the Lord and from the majesty of His power." In this verse, Bible scholars do not all agree on the length of punishment. Some believe that "everlasting" means permanent, i.e. cannot be recovered from. Others believe that "everlasting" means a single event where the punishment goes on for every person punished continuously forever. It doesn't really matter who is correct regarding these two views, the real issue is that whatever the punishment length, we should do what we are asked to do by God to avoid it!

Hades, or Hell, (these terms refer to the same place) is where there is significant torment. When our earthly physical bodies die, our soul will go to heaven if we have believed in God and have been obedient to His commands. If we have not believed and have been disobedient to His commands, our soul will travel to Hell. The scripture that best confirms this is found in the book of Luke, chapter 16, verses 19-28, which reads, "There was a rich man who was dressed in purple and fine linen and lived in luxury every day. At his gate was laid a beggar named Lazarus, covered with sores and longing to eat what fell from the rich man's table. Even the dogs came and licked his sores.

The time came when the beggar died and the angels carried him to Abraham's side. The rich man also died and was buried. In Hades, where he was in torment, he looked up and saw Abraham far away, with Lazarus by his side. So he called to him, 'Father Abraham, have pity on me and send Lazarus to dip the tip of his finger in water and cool my tongue, because I am in agony in this fire.'

But Abraham replied, 'Son, remember that in your lifetime you received your good things, while Lazarus received bad things, but now he is comforted here and you are in agony. And besides all this, between us and you a great chasm has been set in place, so that those who want to go from here to you cannot, nor can anyone cross over from there to us.' He answered, 'Then I beg you, father, send Lazarus to my family, for I have five brothers. Let him warn them, so that they will not also come to this place of torment.'" The rich man did not lead a life pleasing to God. His soul, upon physical death, departed for Hell. Hell is not eternal. After Jesus returns and reigns for one thousand years (Revelation, chapter 19), Satan is released from Hell and then cast into the lake of fire and will be tormented day and night forever (Revelation, chapter 20). Subsequent to that, God will judge all men and women. If we have been obedient, we move from the current heaven to the new heaven.

If we have not been obedient, we move from Hell into the lake of fire along with Hell and death itself. This is referred to as the second death from which there is no way to recover. Putting together the revelation of truth about the fate of the unrepentant souls tends to lead us to the view that souls are consumed in the lake of fire, unlike Satan's fate which is perpetual. Proof that God is capable of the extinguishment of both a person's physical body and soul is found in the book of Matthew, chapter 10, verse 28, as God tells us, "Do not be afraid of those who kill the body but cannot kill the soul. Rather, be afraid of the One who can destroy both soul and body in hell." The reference to "the One" refers to God the Father. He clearly has the ability to destroy physical bodies and spiritual souls. For those whom this destruction occurs (because of a person's disobedience and unrepentance and/or a person's unbelief), the only issue is the timing, which we have already discussed. So, whether punishment ends in the lake of fire or continues forever, the fact is it will be unpleasant.

There is one remaining thought to share regarding eternal life. God is going to replace earth with a new earth and He is going to place the new Jerusalem, the Holy City, Heaven itself (all terms for the same place), on the new earth. The scripture to support this is in the book of Revelation, chapter 21, verses 1-5, as follows, "Then I saw a new heaven and a new earth, for the first heaven and the first earth had passed away, and there was no longer any sea. I saw the Holy City, the new Jerusalem, coming down out of heaven from God, prepared as a bride beautifully dressed for her husband. And I heard a loud voice from the throne saying, 'Look! God's dwelling place is now among the people, and he will dwell with them. They will be his people, and God himself will be with them and be their God. He will wipe every tear from their eyes. There will be no more death or mourning or crying or pain, for the old order of things has passed away.' He who was seated on the throne said, 'I am making everything new!' Then he said, 'Write this down, for these words are trustworthy and true.'" This passage should be one of the most encouraging and exciting in all of scripture for the believer. God is not only telling the believer that He will create a perfect place to live forever, but He will be there! While you hear people use the phrase, "It doesn't get better than that", the use of it in reference to eternity with God is actually the one and only time it is true!

As this chapter comes to a close, let's summarize a few important points:

When our physical bodies die, our soul goes to heaven or hell.

On the day of judgement, our soul stays in heaven or, if our soul has been in hell it is now is cast into the lake of fire along with the rest of hell. Satan goes first.

A new earth is created.

The new heaven/Jerusalem/Holy City/God's dwelling place is placed on the new earth. God will reside there and so will we as long as we believe in Him and repent of our sins.

Thinking about life after death can be interesting for some and a bit scary for others. Many choose to ignore what may happen after our physical bodies die. Once you know the truth, however, thinking about the reality of life after death is exciting!

Scripture contains the truth and exists to teach us, rebuke us, correct us, and encourage us. The truth about life after death is revealed to us in scripture. The final chapter of this book will address spending time with God as well as miracles we experience. Both of these subjects, when experienced, will solidify our relationship with God. The first, by strengthening our understanding of who He is and the second, by witnessing firsthand how the impossible becomes possible because of who God is.

CHAPTER 12

Spending Time with God and Miracles

Spending time with God is something many believers do not make a high priority. A reason for this is that we cannot see Him. To us, He exists only in the spiritual dimension, that is, until we take our last breath on earth. However, with proper focus while still on earth, it is easy to see much evidence of God. That evidence is all around us. The world God created contains so much beauty. The world also contains some wonderful animals, plants, oceans, fish, mountains, and much more that amaze us. Just looking up at the sky at night should remind us of how large the universe is and, as the Bible says in the book of Psalms, chapter 19, verse 1, "The heavens declare the glory of God; the skies proclaim the work of His hands." It is not hard to be reminded every day of our great God. On top of recognizing God daily because of what He has created (including us!), we should never forget the sacrifice He made for us. He came to earth in physical form and literally suffered a painful death for us. That should motivate us to not only be enormously thankful but to want to spend time with Him.

One way to spend time with God is to read scripture, i.e. the Word of God. Reading His Word is a decision each individual makes. If you have faith in God, there is no valid reason not to spend time reading God's Word. Reading His Word strengthens us, provides wisdom, and enables us to be prepared to share the truth with others. Think about the time you first fell in love. Let's assume you wrote a love letter to the person whom you loved. The letter was given to this person and the person knew the letter was from you. Let's further assume that the person whom you wrote the letter to said they loved you, but never opened the letter. The person said the reason they did not open and read the letter is that they have been too busy, or that they don't need to read it because they already know you and know how you feel. How would that make you feel? Now think about how God feels if, for the same reasons, we ignore His love letter to us (His Word/scripture). Our gratefulness to God for creating us and loving us should be continuous. We should want to please Him and demonstrate our love for Him by our actions. One of those actions is to spend time with Him. Reading His Word is spending time with Him. Don't fall into the trap of not making time for God due to the busyness of life. There are very few people who are immune to being busy. Essentially, folks who are retired may be free from the tyranny of busyness. Although, even many retired people fill their time such that spending time with God is crowded out be less essential tasks. For those in the workforce, being busy is almost a guarantee. Add to a full-time job raising children and the fullness of each day can become overwhelming. When thinking about your daily "to do" list, making time for God doesn't even typically appear in the top 10. We must prioritize spending time with God. One practice that works for many is spending time with God at a certain time of day every day. Some people do this with exercising, eating, sleeping, and going to work or school. If it can be done with these tasks, it can certainly be done with spending time with God. We could make a daily commitment to reading His Word at a time of day that is most convenient. The morning seems to work well for many as the time spent with God can be completed before we get immersed in the tasks of life that require attention. You do not have to read God's Word for two hours per day, but a small amount of time consistently is well worth the effort. The same is true for any behavior that is good for us. Whatever time of day may work for you, developing the daily habit of spending time reading God's Word is essential to reaping the benefits of gaining wisdom to apply to your life, understanding God better, and realizing the deepest experience of God possible while on earth. Of course, there are other ways to spend time with God that result in capturing the same benefits and should also be pursued.

Spending time with God can be done by reading His Word, but we can also spend time with God by talking to Him (which you can do continually). The more you talk to God, the more you will experience Him and your ability to hear the Holy Spirit will clearly be sharpened. The latter is a bit confusing as you may wonder, "If am talking to God how can I hear Him?" The answer is two-fold. First, when you talk to God, He will answer. That may occur instantaneously, or at a future point in time. When He answers, you will hear Him. His answers most commonly come in the form of circumstances that occur at some point after we have prayed which are specifically related to our prayer. Secondly, the Holy Spirit often communicates to us as we pray, just like He does when we are not praying. For example, the Holy Spirit may bring a particular person to your mind while you are praying. You have the urge to pray for that person but may or may not know why that person needs prayer. There is nothing wrong with praying for someone without full knowledge of why the person needs prayer. God knows all about the circumstances in the person's life whom you are praying for and that is more than enough. Additional discussion of the Holy Spirit speaking to us as we pray will be addressed in the next paragraph.

Many people believe talking to God works best when you are alone in a quiet place without distractions. Others think you need to talk to God by praying specific prayers. Both are correct. Jesus gave us instructions regarding how to pray. Those appear in the book of Matthew, chapter 6, verses 5-13, where God tells us, "And when you pray, do not be like the hypocrites, for they love to pray standing in the synagogues and on the street corners to be seen by others. Truly I tell you, they have received their reward in full. But when you pray, go into your room, close the door and pray to your Father, who is unseen. Then your Father, who sees what is done in secret, will reward you. And when you pray, do not keep on babbling like pagans, for they think they will be heard because of their many words. Do not be like them, for your Father knows what you need before you ask him. This, then, is how you should pray: Our Father in heaven, hallowed be your name, your kingdom come, your will be done, on earth as it is in heaven. Give us today our daily bread. And forgive us our debts, as we also have forgiven our debtors. And lead us not into temptation, but deliver us from the evil one." The passage indicates that praying in the synagogue or on a street corner for others to see how "holy" a person may be is hypocritical. To avoid that, praying in privacy or away from crowds is recommended. Jesus did just that as referenced many times in the Bible. Three such references are found in the book of Matthew, chapter 14, verses 22-23, the book of Mark, chapter 1, verse 35, and the book of Luke, chapter 6, verse 12. The text for the book of Matthew reference is, "Immediately Jesus made the disciples get into the boat and go on ahead of Him to the other side, while He dismissed the crowd. After He had dismissed them, He went up on a mountainside by Himself to pray." The text for the book of Mark reference is, "Very early in the morning, while it was still dark, Jesus got up, left the house and went off to a solitary place, where He prayed." The text for the book of Luke reference is, "One of those days Jesus went out to a mountainside to pray, and spent the night praying to God." These are examples of

Jesus going to a place away from people to pray. The benefits of praying in private are not just to avoid being hypocritical. The other benefits of praying in private are two-fold. First, you will be undistracted and have clarity of thought. Secondly, you will be better able to listen to Him when He speaks to you. Yes, God speaks to us and often. When God speaks to us it is through His Holy Spirit. The Holy Spirit comes to dwell within us alongside our spirit. The Holy Spirit continuously speaks to our spirit. We do not always hear the Holy Spirit or attribute certain thoughts to being from Him. Some people refer to listening to the Holy Spirit as paying attention to the still small voice that we hear within us. How do we know God speaks to us through His Holy Spirit? In the book of John, chapter 16, verses 13-15 God tells us, "But when He, the Spirit of truth, comes, He will guide you into all the truth. He will not speak on His own; He will speak only what He hears, and He will tell you what is yet to come. He will glorify me because it is from me that He will receive what He will make known to you. All that belongs to the Father is mine. That is why I said the Spirit will receive from me what He will make known to you." Many people have difficulty knowing that what they hear is really the voice of God through His Holy Spirit. Over time, it becomes easier to recognize the Holy Spirit's promptings to us. The better equipped you are with knowledge of the Word of God, the easier it will be to hear the Holy Spirit. The reason is the Word of God is God and the Holy Spirit is God. Therefore, what you hear from the Holy Spirit will be in sync with the Word of God.

Praying for specific things is good, but keep in mind that God already knows your heart and every thought you have. We do not need to help God by informing Him of something we do not think He knows. Having said that, all our prayers are listened to by God regardless of the being specific or general in the words we use. In the passage of prayer instructions in the book of Matthew, chapter 6, Jesus is telling us of the important elements of prayer, i.e., the types of things we should pray about. Inasmuch as God already knows our every thought, prayer is to be used to acknowledge to God that we depend upon Him for everything including provision in our lives and spiritual protection from the devil. Forgiveness is given special attention in the instructions Jesus gave us regarding how to pray. We need Him to enable us to forgive by the power of His love, which we covered earlier in this book.

In addition to reading His Word, talking to God, and listening to God, we are also spending time with God when we love others. Yes, when you love others you are spending time with God because it is His Holy Spirit that enables you to love. The only way we can truly love others with His agape love is through the work of the Holy Spirit. Therefore, we are spending time with God as He works through us while we love others. This was covered earlier in the book but important and relevant to be reiterated here.

All of the ways we spend time with God are extremely beneficial to us. To summarize, those benefits are to gain wisdom, get to know Him better, be strengthened spiritually, be prepared to share the truth with other people, be filled with peace, and experience much joy.

The final topic of this book is miracles. A discussion of miracles will be of interest to many, but reactions to the subject are dependent upon a person's world view. For example, an atheist would have no reason to believe in miracles inasmuch as to believe in miracles would mean believing in the source of miracles, or at the very least, be curious about the source of a miracle. This line of thinking would inevitably lead to God, or some supernatural power. Heading down that path is not usually in an atheist thinker's playbook. The reason is simple. There is quite a dilemma created when an atheist minded person experiences a miracle in their life. Typically, when this occurs, the atheist minded person has only one approach to thinking about the circumstances that appeared miraculous. The atheist explains the miracle as a major coincidence without giving credit to God, who was the person behind the miracle.

A miracle is defined in the Merriam-Webster dictionary as, "an extraordinary event manifesting divine intervention in human affairs." The Oxford dictionary defines a miracle as, "a surprising and welcome event that is not explicable by natural or scientific laws and is therefore considered to be the work of a divine agency." Both definitions imply that something is orchestrated with supernatural assistance. There are countless instances of doctors who cannot explain how a person survived a serious health event. Some doctors just admit that they were wrong or misjudged the severity of the circumstances and, after the patient recovers, believes the patient was not in as critical a situation as originally thought. Some doctors believe the patient's will to live enabled the patient to defeat the odds and survive. Other doctors, however, do believe that there are cases where only God's intervention could have healed a person. You can certainly provide an educated guess regarding the world view of each of these groups of doctors. These various beliefs or cerebral postures a person takes when encountering a miracle isn't limited to doctors' opinions, but extends to every human being when presented with events that occur which are unexplainable as they occur outside of natural laws.

Many people focus on miraculous healings as the primary form of miracles. Jesus healed many people of their physical ailments during His time on earth. Folks who were blind then began to see, those who were crippled then began to walk, those with leprosy were healed, a woman who had a constant flow of blood was healed, Jesus put an ear back on a soldier that had been cut off, and multiple folks who had died came back to life! No one would argue that all of these events in Jesus' life are miracles. Looking beyond physical body healings, we also learned that Jesus cast demons out of people, fed thousands of people with five loaves of bread and two fish, and fed thousands on another occasion with a few loaves of bread, turned water into wine at a wedding reception, walked on water (the Sea of Galilee), calmed a storm by telling it to stop, helped the disciples have miraculous fishing expeditions (once they caught more fish than they thought possible, the other occasion was when a fish was caught with money in its mouth to pay their taxes), and Jesus withered a fig tree. Whether the miracle was a physical body healing or something other than directly related to a physical body, all miracles defy our ability to comprehend how they took place. This is a very important concept inasmuch as we are going to explore many other kinds of miracles that fit the criteria of our inability to understand how something miraculous happened in our life, much less our ability to cause the miracle to take place. As we discuss miracles the primary issue will be whether or not you attribute the miracle to God.

Is there anything God cannot do? Yes, there is something God cannot do. He cannot sin. Other than that, God can do anything. We have identified many miracles God carried out during His time on earth in the person of Jesus. There are also examples of miracles God the Father carried out while in heaven. There is some debate regarding precisely how these miracles were performed (by God the Father from heaven or through the Holy Spirit dispatched to earth). Determining whether God the Father or the Holy Spirit performed the miracle is not important, however, knowing God performed the miracles is important and is what we should focus upon. These miracles include parting the Red Sea, protecting Shadrach, Meshach, and Abednego when thrown into the fiery furnace, protecting Daniel when he was thrown into the lion's pit, the ten plagues sent to Egypt, raining manna (bread) for the Israelites, water flowing from a rock in the desert of Zin, Balaam's donkey speaking, flooding the entire earth, and the sun and moon standing still. There are many more, but this list gives you a good understanding of the magnitude of the miracles God carried out, even while the person of Jesus was in heaven rather than on earth.

Given the types of miracles Jesus (God) performed while on earth and the miracles God performed when Jesus was not walking the earth, we realize that none of these miracles can be explained by coincidence and all of these miracles required supernatural intervention, hence, we confidently categorize the events as miracles. Since we do not need to be convinced that God *can* perform a miracle, our next objective is to understand whether or not God intervenes when we ask Him and performs miracles in our lives. There is no doubt He tells us to ask. However, asking God is not informing God of our need. He already knows. To reiterate what we reviewed in the discussion of prayer, in the book of Matthew, chapter 6, verse 8, God tells us, "Do not be like them, for your Father knows what you need before you ask Him." He doesn't want us to ramble as if the more we say the more likely He is to grant our request (see Matthew, chapter 6, verse 7). He wants us to acknowledge to Him in prayer that we recognize our need and the fact that we need Him to intervene. In the book of Matthew, chapter 7, verses 7-8, God tells us, "Ask and it will be given to you; seek and you will find; knock and the door will be opened." In the book of John, chapter 14, verses 13-14, God says, "And I will do whatever you ask in my name, so that the Son may bring glory to the Father. You may ask me for anything in my name, and I will do it." This seems like a huge open door God has given us. There, however, are a couple of conditions to be satisfied regarding what we ask and how God responds.

The first condition is for our prayers to align with God's will. When Jesus taught us how to pray, chronicled in the book of Matthew, chapter 6, He made it clear that we are to pray for God's will to be done. In chapter 8 of this book, we acquired a thorough understanding of God's will. This understanding will actually help ensure that when we pray, our prayers will be on point regarding God's will. For example, we learned that God's will is for us to pursue holiness and, therefore, avoid evil. If, during our time of prayer, we ask to be forgiven of our sins and given a more holy mindset, God will intervene on our behalf to help us. How can we be certain He will intervene? Because our prayer is His will. Let's look at another example. He tells us that He will provide for our basic needs. He tells us how He feeds the birds and that He is even more willing to care for us. So, if we pray for provision to meet the basic needs in our lives or the lives of others, He will intervene and provide. Again, we can be confident that He will intervene because what we are asking Him for is His will. His intervention certainly qualifies as miraculous given His supernatural actions are activated. You may have experienced His intervention regarding provision in your life or have witnessed it in the life of someone you know. Most people on earth have received consistent provision for basic needs from God. In fact, many have received provision without ever asking God for it or thanking Him for it. So, why pray and ask for provision? The answer is that our prayers will not be ignored by God and when He responds to our prayers there will always be supernatural intervention specifically aimed at how we prayed. For example, if a person was just laid off from a job and needed another job, prayer for God to provide an open door to the next job will ensure that the next job is best for the individual who prayed. The previous statement doesn't mean that if a person does not pray for their next job opportunity that the next job they find will not be a good job. What is does mean is when we pray, God's intervention guarantees the next job is the best job for the person at that time in their life because God had a hand in orchestrating the events to make it happen.

Another example of praying for God's will is when we pray for someone we know to connect with God. We know from our discussion earlier in the book that God's will is that no one will perish. If we pray for a person who does not believe in God to acknowledge that He exists and begin a relationship with Him, that would seem consistent with God's will. Of course it is. And, God will intervene. However, unlike provision, salvation remains governed by the will of every individual. Any person, regardless of the promptings of God or events in their life that point them in the direction of God, can still reject Him. In other words, God can and will answer our prayers for the salvation of others through His actions in the lives of those we pray for, however, God will not force the person we pray for to make the decision to believe. He tells us it is each person's choice to believe or not believe. The ability to have this choice is called free will. Furthermore, we do not know who will believe and who will not believe. Therefore, we should not limit whom we pray for by attempting to determine who is likely to believe. If we pray for a person's salvation, God intervenes, and because of that intervention they begin to believe in God, we can rejoice and thank God for what He did. If we pray for a person's salvation, God intervenes, and if the person does not believe, now or ever, we can still thank God for what He did. He is always faithful to His promises to answer our prayers that are in accordance with His will. God's action was the same regarding answering our prayer for the unbeliever. God's action was not predicated upon His knowledge of the unbeliever's ultimate choice to believe or not.

In each of these examples of praying for God's will, He intervenes because we have fulfilled one of the conditions by which we know He will intervene, that is praying for His will to be done. However, there is a second condition that must exist for God to intervene. The second condition is the belief, without any doubt, of the person praying that God can intervene, and will intervene. In the book of Mark, chapter 11, verse 24, God tells us, "Therefore I tell you, whatever you ask for in prayer, believe that you have received it, and it will be yours." There are folks who read this scripture and apply it without limits. In other words, some people believe that if they ask for a new jet and believe they will receive it, that they better start taking pilot lessons and purchasing jet fuel. Remember, **both** conditions must be met. Our prayer has to be in accordance with God's will **and** we must believe that it will happen. If there is no need for a new jet in our lives other than to make our travel more comfortable or efficient, it is unlikely that God will intervene and provide a new jet. On the other hand, if a person is responsible for running a large organization that transports Bibles and food throughout the world, it is very likely that God will provide a new jet that the organization needs inasmuch as the organization's purpose is consistent with God's will. The need, in the latter case, qualifies as a real, tangible need to carry out God's will. The need in the former case qualifies as a want rather than an essential need. There are many other examples of praying for wants versus needs. Continuing on the subject of provision, most of us agree having a place to live (shelter) is a need. However, the *type* of place to live can vary tremendously. If you are single, a nice studio apartment meets the need. If you are married and have two children, a three bedroom home easily meets the need. If you were to ask God to intervene to provide a place to live that meets your need and you believe He can, He will. If you were to ask God to intervene to provide an eight bedroom, seven bathroom home and you are either single or have a modest size family, you are asking for a want rather than a need. If, however, you desire to open your home to people in transition (temporarily displaced from a home) or those whom have real need of a place to live, then the large home you are asking for becomes a need since it is associated with the social service you are attempting to provide.

The underlying reason behind a person's request to God is largely influenced by whether or not the person is focused on God or focused on themselves. In the previous example, providing a place to live that will meet the needs of others is clearly indicative of a person focused on God rather than themselves. There are many scripture that define taking care of the poor, widows, and orphans as something we should all do, and doing so is loving the person or people we are helping. As we learned earlier in this book, when we love another person we are doing God's will. When we attempt to do God's will and ask for His help, He never ignores our request. To drive the point home, let's assume that a father asks his son to clean out the garage. The father has been wanting the garage cleaned for a awhile and has not had the opportunity to address the garage due to a heavy work schedule. If the son cheerfully agrees to tackle the task, and asks the father for a few needed items (such as a broom and some work gloves, most father's would not ignore the son's request. The same is true of God. We are His children and when we attempt to carry out something He asks of us, He will respond to our requests. Let's examine a few other examples of praying for God to intervene.

The next example is of a couple who have been married for 12 years. A significant amount of strife has developed in the marriage. One of the members of this marriage (the woman) is connected to God and pursuing holiness. The other person (the man) in this marriage wants nothing whatsoever to do with God and has a hardening heart toward his spouse. If the woman in this marriage begins to pray that God will intervene and soften her husband's heart, and believes that it will happen, God will intervene to ensure the circumstances (for example, people her husband encounters) will take place designed to help soften his heart. However, although the human heart can be deeply influenced by God, every human has the free will to deny God access. In other words, the husband in our example has the ability to choose to continue to be closed off to God. God does not take the ability to choose away from any person. The wife who has prayed for her husband has not prayed in vain. Her prayers were certainly heard and responded to by God. Her husband will receive the supernaturally orchestrated events in his life designed to answer his wife's prayers. How the husband responds is entirely his choice.

When we pray for others, particularly for someone to acknowledge God and receive salvation, the fact that the person may continue to reject God should never discourage us in terms of doubting that the outcome we want is possible. In fact, the enemy uses discouragement to paralyze our ability to pray by convincing us that what we want to pray for is unlikely to occur. That is why it is essential never to relinquish the belief that what we pray for will happen. When we cease to believe, we will be less likely to pray, or we will pray and subsequently become discouraged when our prayers seem to yield no results.

When most people think of miracles, they think with their eyes. They see something extraordinary occur that cannot be explained by worldly circumstances. There is nothing wrong with that thinking. However, many miracles occur that we cannot see with our eyes. For example, let's assume you routinely pray for physical protection over your family and the following occurs. One day, your family is on a driving road trip. Along the way you are unexpectedly delayed for about an hour. As you continue on the trip, you encounter a massive amount of traffic. This traffic developed because of a major accident. The accident occurred about an hour before you arrived to that point along the highway. Do you believe the unexpected delay could have been the reason your family was not involved in the accident? You may think that the timing of your delay and the accident was just a coincidence. These types of "coincidences" occur often. If the outcome of a set of circumstances is consistent with a prayer you have uttered, and the outcome happened because of other unplanned events, it is more likely than not that God intervened. Please know that I am not suggesting that there are never coincidences when God does not intervene, but rather we should be keenly aware of what we have prayed for and notice the coincidences that surround circumstances related to our prayers.

If you look back at the circumstances in your life I am confident that you will find examples that you could label as coincidences or you could attribute the circumstances to the intervention of God. Let's look at another example. This example is that of two people who became married. One was born in New York City in the State of New York. The other was born in San Antonio, Texas. The person born in New York moved to Phoenix, Arizona, then Fort Worth, Texas, then Lakewood, California, then Mission Viejo, California, then Exeter, California, then Long Beach, California, then Galena, Ohio, then San Antonio, Texas. The two people who became husband and wife met in San Antonio, Texas, ten years after the person born in New York, then moved many times to different places in the United States, landed in San Antonio. Along the way, there were literally hundreds of decisions made and circumstances encountered that led the person born in New York to end up in San Antonio. Furthermore, the person born in New York was married for many years before his first wife, who now dwells in heaven, passed away. During the year subsequent to his wife's physical death, he met the woman born in San Antonio, whom would become his wife a couple of years later. The woman who was born in San Antonio was raised in Lytle, Texas. After high school, she left Lytle and went to school in Brownwood, Texas. After college, she moved back to San Antonio. She considered moving to New Mexico and asked God to provide a job in San Antonio confirming that she should stay. A few days before she was to leave San Antonio and relocate to New Mexico, she found a very good job in San Antonio.

Being cognizant of the many circumstances both people encountered in life, would you conclude meeting each other in San Antonio was a random event? One that God had nothing to do with? Here are additional facts that may help shed light upon these questions. Both the woman born in San Antonio and the man born in New York prayed for God to orchestrate events that would bring them a companion for life whom shared their values and faith. You may initially think that meeting each other could have happened without God's intervention. What if one of them was not living in San Antonio, but they still met, and subsequently married? We could add additional facts that would keep decreasing the likelihood of the two people meeting. Whatever facts we could add that decrease the likelihood of the two people meeting does not change the degree of difficulty for God since He can do all things. How do we acknowledge that God intervened? The most certain way is to pray about everything and observe what happens. When there are circumstances that exist that make it is obvious a miracle is needed, and then the miracle happens, you can be sure God answered your prayer.

In our example, God knew the two people would marry even before either of them was born. It is entirely possible that God orchestrated events throughout their lives that would bring them both to San Antonio and see to it that they met. One of the more difficult attributes of God for us to understand is that there are no constraints nor limitations to what He knows. That includes the constraints or limitations related to time. Since humans think in finite terms, it is hard for us to comprehend what God is capable of, how He transcends time, and how He is all knowing. Let me share one final fact regarding the example of the two folks born in different parts of the country whom met and married in San Antonio. This is not a hypothetical story. These two people are Melissa and I. We lived this miracle. And, for the past eleven years we have enjoyed the blessings of companionship with the foundation of our relationship being the one true God.

Let's reiterate a very important point regarding how to recognize that God intervened. There are many stories that contain facts with odds that indicate a particular outcome is very unlikely. Herein lies the irony. For people whom have prayed to God for Him to intervene in some way, the more unlikely that the outcome that was prayed for would occur, the more likely God was involved if that outcome did occur.

We have explored spending time with God and miracles in Chapter 12. This is the final chapter of the book. Before this chapter and book come to a close, there is a challenge offered. Regardless of your age, look back on your life and reflect on situations where a specific outcome may have seemed impossible. Then find some of those situations when the specific outcome desired did, in fact, occur. Also, try to recall if you prayed for the outcome you desired. If you did pray, those prayers activated God to intervene given the conditions laid out earlier in this chapter. As you reflect upon your past in this way, you will soon begin to accumulate memories of the many miracles in your life. These miracles do not have to be as phenomenal as some of the miracles Jesus performed when He walked the earth, but God is nonetheless involved in the miracle.

There are also miracles in our life that exist without prayer. To qualify as a miracle there must be supernatural intervention in an area of our life. I can confidently say that every person has experienced a miracle. Life itself is a miracle. When you examine how humans are created, the billions of instructions held within the initial cells of our body, and exactly what takes place to form our bodies, those facts should make anyone marvel at our great God. The creation of life requires supernatural intervention. The fact that you are reading this book is a miracle. Think of every action that took place to make this moment possible. Combine those thoughts with the fact that the content of the book is solely focused on deciphering what truth is, who God is, and whom love is. If you believe the truth you have read, you will acknowledge that God exists and that God is love, if you are being intellectually honest. You will also realize that understanding truth is a supernatural event and an exciting privilege. How can I say that? Because understanding the truth is equivalent to understanding revelation from God. Understanding is orchestrated by God inasmuch as He has revealed truth to us through His word. In Psalm 119, verse 104, God makes it clear how we gain understanding. It is written, "I gain understanding from your precepts; therefore, I hate every wrong path." The word "precepts" in this verse refers to a command or principle that is a general rule governing our actions. Our understanding of the truth occurs as we read God's instructions for living. In the book of 1 John, chapter 5, verse 20, God tells us that, "We know also that the Son of God has come and has given us understanding, so that we may know Him who is true." This verse continues but what has been captured here is enough to make the point that understanding spiritual truth comes from God. In the book of Isaiah, chapter 11, verse 2, God is talking about David when He says, "The Spirit of the Lord will rest on him- the Spirit of wisdom and of understanding, the Spirit of counsel and of power, the Spirit of knowledge and of the fear of the Lord." Here is more reinforcement of the truth that God (in this verse, the Holy Spirit) will convey understanding. Knowing that God gives us understanding should motivate us to spend time with Him (the subject matter from earlier in this chapter). If you desire to find truth, you must seek it. If you desire to not just be aware of truth but **understand** truth, you must seek understanding through God who is the source of truth.

There are two outcomes to believing or not believing the truth. If a person does not believe the truth, he/she will believe an untruth, or lie. In the book of Romans, chapter 1, verse 25, God describes these unbelievers when He says, "They have exchanged the truth of God for a lie, and worshipped and served created things rather than the Creator-who is forever praised. Amen." A person could be seeking the truth and fail to believe the truth even when confronted with it. A person may not be seeking the truth or believes they already know the truth so when they see or hear the truth, it is not accepted. What a person who does not accept the truth doesn't realize, is that they, in fact, believe a lie. On the other hand, if a person believes the truth, the acceptance and understanding of the truth not only provides the path to salvation, but empowers us to live a life free from the snare of sin. In the book of John, chapter 8, verses 31-32, God tells us, "If you hold to my teaching, you are really my disciples. Then you will know the truth, and the truth will set you free." Freedom from what? Sin. Sin causes a multitude of problems. Sin separates us from God. We become less productive believers given it is impossible to sin and have God's Agape love flowing through us. Ultimately, not believing the truth keeps us apart from God. If someone never believes the truth while in their earthly bodies, the separation from God becomes permanent. Knowing, understanding, and believing the truth helps empower us to **not** give in to sinful temptations that we encounter each day, and that spiritual strength leads to loving God and others with His Agape love, leading to joy. Knowing the truth alone will not change your life. Knowing and understanding the truth will not change your life. Knowing, understanding, **and** believing is what activates God's truths within your soul. Hence, belief in the truth is vital to experiencing all that God has made possible for us. If we know that fact, you can bet our adversary, Satan, knows that fact. He attempts to distract us from seeing the truth clearly inasmuch as he knows if we see the truth clearly, there is a good chance we will understand and believe the truth. Satan lies to us daily. How do I know that Satan lies to us? Read what God tells us about Satan in the book of John, chapter 8, verse 44, "You belong to your father, the devil, and you want to carry out your father's desire. He was a murderer from the beginning, not holding to the truth, for there is no truth in him. When he lies, he speaks his native language, for he is a liar and the father of lies."

A few examples will demonstrate the need for knowledge, understanding and belief to be present for a person to realize the benefits of the truth. Let's assume a person becomes aware of the fact that something called electricity gives energy to turn lights on in our homes, keeps the refrigerator running, etc. Let's further assume that an electrician explains how electricity works, and the dangers inherent in our direct contact with electricity. Since we have knowledge of electricity (what it is), and understanding of electricity (how it works), if we believe what the electrician told us regarding the potential harm electricity could cause us, we will take measures to protect ourselves from direct interaction with electricity. If we do not believe what the electrician told us regarding potential harm from electricity, we will be less cautious around electricity. The result of the latter behavior could be harmful, or (worst case scenario) fatal to us.

The second example is in the world of art. As a person experiences life, they become aware that transferring images from their mind to paper or canvas is called art (gains knowledge). As the person explores more about art, they learn that they can use various colors of paint to create a picture on a canvas (gains understanding). If the person does not believe the truth, they will never try to paint a picture. If the person does believe the truth, they will engage in painting and the result will be enlightening and personal growth.

The third example is related to spiritual truth. Let's assume a person becomes aware (gains knowledge) that there are many who profess that there is a God. Furthermore, the same person then learns (gains understanding) who God is, what He has done for us, and how we can be with Him forever. This same person will decide whether or not they believe in God. If they believe in God (a spiritual truth), they will obey Him and be with Him forever. If they do not believe in God, they will not care about obeying Him and will be separated from God and punished. All of these examples intentionally highlighted the danger of not believing and activating the truth within ourselves.

You can see how several of the concepts presented throughout this book are interconnected. Most truths are interconnected. In fact, as you learn more truths, the interconnectivity of various truths is proof that a particular concept is truth. The more truth you know, understand, and believe, the broader your view of reality. It is likely no coincidence that the Hebrew word for truth, אמת (pronounced eh-MEHT) begins with the first letter of the Hebrew alphabet, has one of two middle letters of the Hebrew alphabet as its' second letter, and ends with the last letter of the Hebrew alphabet. The aggregation of all truth encompasses the totality of reality. If it were possible to know all truth, you would know all reality. Non-truth is not reality. If a person believes a non-truth, they are believing something that is wrong and not real.

If a person believes a single truth, they are believing something that explains a portion of reality. One truth is that bees collect nectar.

What they do with the nectar is another truth. Bees also collect pollen. What they do with the pollen is another truth. If a person believes that gasoline is refined from oil and oil is pulled from inside the earth, they are believing a truth. On the other hand, if a person believes the tooth fairy exists, they are believing an untruth. If a person believes human beings can fly without the aid of an airplane or some other flying mechanism, they are believing an untruth. If a person believes the Grand Canyon does not exist, they are believing an untruth. If a person believes fire will not hurt you, they are believing an untruth. The examples contained in this paragraph seem simplistic, however, remember that people will choose to believe almost anything. We make decisions every day to believe or disbelieve a truth. Many of the decisions we make have no serious ramifications in our lives. However, there are many truths that do have serious ramifications in our lives. That is why this book was written.

The sincere hope is that the truths revealed through the pages of this book will help many see the truth more clearly. In addition, and of equal importance, as people see the truth more clearly, they also see untruth more clearly and recognize the untruth as untruth. If you think about counterfeit money, the more you know about what real money looks like and the attributes of real money, the easier it is to identify the counterfeit, or fake, money. You can apply this concept to any truth and untruth.

Your quest to know, understand, and believe the truth will be aided by your diligence in pursuing deep understanding of single truths and interconnecting those truths. As you interconnect truths you are simultaneously eliminating the belief in untruths related to the subject you are studying. Every encounter you have with truth will help you grow, if that encounter is composed of knowledge, understanding, and belief. In the book of Isaiah, chapter 55, verses 10-11, God tells us that, "As the rain and the snow come down from heaven, and do not return to it without watering the earth and making it bud and flourish, so that it yields seed for the sower and bread for the eater, so is My work that goes out from My mouth: It will not return to Me empty, but will accomplish what I desire and achieve the purpose for which I sent it." As an author of this book, this passage from the book of Isaiah leads to much joy knowing that each person who spends time reading this book will be exposed to knowledge and understanding of the truth, while recognizing that belief in the truths presented in this book are the choice of each person. Please consider each truth carefully before accepting or rejecting it. In addition, before accepting or rejecting a truth, look for corroboration based upon the interconnectedness of the truths contained in this book. By virtue of the interconnectedness of truths presented in this book, you can see God is truth, God is love, and truth is love. Lastly, pray for discernment of truth and for guidance from God. He will never let you down.

www.ingramcontent.com/pod-product-compliance
Lightning Source LLC
Chambersburg PA
CBHW071239070526
44583CB00017B/2244